QUESTIONS OF THE HEART

LEANING IN, LISTENING FOR, AND LOVING
WELL TOWARD TRUE IDENTITY IN CHRIST

KEVIN THUMPSTON

Published by White Blackbird Books, an imprint of Storied Publishing

Copyright ©2020 by Kevin Thumpston

Permission requests and other questions may be directed to the Contact page at www.storied.pub.

Unless otherwise indicated, Scripture quotations are from the ESV Bible (The Holy Bible, English Standard Version), copyright 2001 by Crossway, a publishing ministry of Good News Publishers. 2011 Text Edition. All rights reserved.

ISBN: 978-1-951991-05-0

Cover design by Sean Benesh

IN PRAISE OF QUESTIONS OF THE HEART

Questions of the Heart is conversational, draws from a wide, rich batch of cultural resources, and it's biblical. I'm grateful for Kevin's zeal to bring the practice of thoughtful evangelism to the forefront.

Sandra McCracken

Singer songwriter

Looking for an effective resource to spur conversation with colleagues, friends, and family members about how Jesus satisfies the deepest longings of the human heart? Kevin has provided an excellent resource. *Questions* of the Heart will help.

Scott Sauls

Pastor, Christ Presbyterian Church, Nashville, Tennessee

Author, *A Gentle Answer*

In *Questions of the Heart* Kevin Thumpston tells an array of stories, including his own. He leads us into all of the most basic questions of life and discipleship. *Questions of the Heart* is readable and wise, a great book for individuals and groups who want to explore the faith or to deepen the faith that is already theirs.

Dan Doriani

Vice President, Covenant Theological Seminary

Author, *Work: It's Purpose, Dignity, and Transformation*

Kevin Thumpston provides an outstanding construct that brings excellent content to the context of evangelism. He creates a venue for introspection that unpacks the individual questions along a continuum of responses with which we all wrestle. This book unearths possibilities for further conversations as one builds a relationship with someone no matter where they are in their faith.

Chris Vogel
Ecosystem Director, Mission to North America

It is a rare thing to meet a pastor who is incredibly thoughtful, faithfully intentional, highly relational, and deeply humble. Kevin is all of the above in the most beautiful way, and I can't wait for you to read his book.

Sammy Rhodes
RUF Campus Minister, University of South Carolina
Author, *Broken and Beloved*

For those who long to see their friends and loved ones come to know Christ, *Questions of the Heart* is a helpful guide. Kevin not only encourages us but shows us how to "flip our approach from asking questions we want this generation to answer to listening for the questions of their hearts and helping them find their answers in Jesus." This book is well worth your study.

David G. Sinclair, Sr.
Pastor, Clemson Presbyterian Church

What is evangelism? How does somebody share a Christ-centered Gospel in such a fragmented world?

Why plant churches if evangelism is not a priority? These are important questions for the Church and the Great Commission today. In *Questions of the Heart,* Kevin engages the lives and stories of many people who feel less than human in this world. Kevin helps us see the challenges ahead of reaching the hearts of the next generation with the Gospel message of grace. I was struck by one fact as I read—this author as planter/pastor has communed with many souls who will last forever! This will be an important resource for many churches seeking to know their communities and invest in the future of church planting.

Clint Wilcke
Catalyst for the Mid-South Church Planting Network

In this practical book, Kevin Thumpston walks alongside you as a mentor and friend while showing you how to connect the heart of God to the heart of someone who doesn't know him. *Questions of the Heart* focuses on knowing and loving the individual, and it is wisely aware of how the Gospel speaks most meaningfully in our cultural moment. This book will help equip you to connect with others and share the greatest news the world has ever known.

Clay Werner
Churchplanter, Pastor
Author, *Gospel Brokenness* and *On The Brink*

I first heard Kevin teach this content at a workshop for church planters who wished for an effective methodology to train their congregations to share their faith. I was so struck that this was not another canned and impersonal tract to memorize that I "stole" the class notes and reproduced them. In Scotland! I might be the first to have carried internationally the admonition to *lean in, listen for, and love well* for a Gospel conversation to your friend's heart. I am sure I will not be the last. The understanding of another person's heart is required if we are to hear their heart cry for the Gospel. Kevin gives us the means to now perceive where our friends are spiritually and where we may begin to invite them to consider Christ. The word is getting out that there is nothing quite like this for encouraging friends to share the heart of Jesus with their friends through winsome questions.

Phil Stogner
Mission to the World, Scotland

Kevin Thumpston handles modern western evangelism with humility and tact, providing a practical way to engage the people in our every day lives with the Gospel. We can't wait to lean in, listen to, and love our friends well this year on campus.

Students of Lifting Lanterns Bible Study
Anderson University

Kevin is uniquely gifted to meet people where they are. He engages them with empathy and grace all the while pointing them to Christ by challenging their assumptions about the world and their place in it. Because he loves God deeply and longs for others to truly know him, Kevin is not content to let those who cross his path drift along in wrong thinking that clouds their vision and potential. In *Questions of the Heart*, Kevin compiles simple techniques in a simple design to equip Christ-followers to enter into the lives of non-Christian friends and acquaintances. As you read, I pray that you will reflect on the questions of your own heart, God's myriad responses to them throughout your life, and that God will ignite in you a desire to engage deeply with others who are still searching for the answers to their heart questions.

AnnMargaret McCraw
CEO at Midlands Orthopaedics & Neurosurgery, P. A.

Tremendous reading. Kevin puts himself out there both spiritually and personally. Lean in, listen and love this book.

John & Kelly Clinger
Owners, Old Mill Brew Pub & Doko Station Pub and Eatery

Kevin teaches me about practically loving your neighbor. In this book, he explains/teaches the reader to listen, to invest and to observe before applying the balm of the Gospel. His observations on our identities serve as a foundation and an important tool for believers as we participate in God's kingdom growth.

D. Wayne Rogers
Principle and Founder, Catalyst Architects
Artist

CONTENTS

To my wife, Andrea, who always listens
to the questions of my heart.

To Andrew, who gave me a love for storytelling.

To Ally, for her missional courage.

To Emma, who challenged me to develop
Questions of the Heart

To Watershed Fellowship, where people are invited to have an
ongoing conversation of the heart

Soli Deo Gloria

ACKNOWLEDGMENTS

Thank you Watershed Fellowship for being a church that encourages every member to follow their kingdom passion. You encouraged me to write this book, which we have been practically piecing together from our inception. We strive to be a church where we can bring our friends and have an ongoing conversation around the questions of our hearts.

Kudos go to Tim and Stephanie Pitzer. Steph created the book's graphics while chasing down three little girls, and Tim gave me margin to act like a writer.

A special thanks to Ted Strawbridge, who believed that Jesus could use this carcass of a man. He challenged me to put my thoughts on paper and gave me opportunities to share them. I miss him and wonder what he is like now in heaven. He was a great friend.

Cheers to all those who previewed *Questions of the Heart* to make it better. Your wisdom and honesty have been good for my soul and my pride. Let's see what the Lord does with it.

Interrobang

A punctuation mark intended to combine the functions
of the question mark and the exclamation mark

A fitting symbol for *Questions of the Heart*

PREFACE

It is a serious thing to live in a society of possible gods
and goddesses, to remember that the dullest most
uninteresting person you can talk to may one day be a
creature which, if you saw it now, you would be
strongly tempted to worship, or else a horror and a
corruption such as you now meet, if at all, only in a
nightmare. All day long we are, in some degree helping
each other to one or the other of these destinations. It
is in the light of these overwhelming possibilities, it is
with the awe and the circumspection proper to them,
that we should conduct all of our dealings with one
another, all friendships, all loves, all play, all politics.
There are no ordinary people.

—C. S. Lewis, *The Weight of Glory*

A young professional in our church once said, "This
church brings out the worst in me." After a deep breath,
she continued, "But I am all the better for it."

Thankfully, she was speaking about how the Gospel

challenged her misplaced identity rather than my poor preaching or pastoral skills. The Gospel has a way of doing that—bringing the worst out of us for our betterment. The same happens when we share the Gospel with others. Our fear, apathy, and shallow understanding is exposed, but our faith, dependence, and love are significantly deepened.

Writing *Questions of the Heart* is my attempt to help those who want to share their faith more. My hope is that it will be a blessing to both my Christian and non-Christian friends, as they wrestle with who they are and find their true identity in Christ.

Questions of the Heart is more of a short guide than a story-formed book. I offer a way to share one's faith with those you do life with from day to day. I didn't want to just persuade my friends to believe what I believe. I wanted to help them discover who they are, or better yet, to know who God is and who they could become through knowing Jesus Christ. Since I love my friends, I want to bless them with helpful handles to take hold of life, to have a framework to build their identity on. Whether they go away thinking more deeply about the challenges they face, rise from their knees with a new identity, or learn how to fight better against ignorance and arrogance, I want to help them go to Jesus with the questions of their faith.

In the first section, you get a glimpse into my thinking. Getting in my head may sound a bit scary, but it will help you understand my motivation behind *Questions of the Heart*.

The second section gets its biblical foundation from

Colossians 4:4–6. There are so many other biblical passages that support sharing your faith, but I chose to focus on this one.

Sections three through five define the terminology and walk you through the *Questions of the Heart* conversation.

Section six shows how Jesus Christ is the answer to all our heart questions and the one in whom we find our true identity.

In section seven, I included Follow-up Conversations with general questions around each identity for you to explore with your friends. In each conversation, you will see Jesus engaging people with similar identity challenges as you and your friends. Your discussions will be helped if you use other biblical helps to go deeper.

In section eight, I tell my own story. I share the questions of my heart along the way of finding my identity in Christ. If we expect our friends to trust us with their story, we need to be willing to reveal the challenges we have faced in our story.

In the last section, I wrap up the book by noting other models on how to share your faith.

We all have questions of the heart, whether we're Christian or not. Our identity is always being challenged. We need to be reminded of our true identity every day. Macaulay and Barrs explain in *Being Human*:

> Very often in fact we are painfully aware of how much our old life is still with us. Our new life is only partially enjoyed at the present because it is "hid with Christ". We will enjoy it to the full when we are

completely new within—only when Christ returns. Until then, we are to grasp in faith the truth that because we are united with Christ, God treats us as his beloved children. Newness, then, though not fully experienced, is already a present possession. Because we belong to Christ, we can even say that the new creation within us is our *true identity* [emphasis mine].[1]

Finding one's true identity is not an existential journey into our best self. You can go to yoga class, read the old philosophers, or watch the latest talk show for that. It's about a radical transformation of who you are —a rebirth, a whole new life united to Christ.

I pray Jesus will use *Questions of the Heart* to help you in some small way to find your true identity in Christ and to help equip you to do the same with your friends.

If you are familiar with Bach, you may know that at the bottom of his manuscripts, he wrote the initials, "S. D. G." *Soli Deo Gloria*, which means, "glory to God alone." What you may not know is that at the top of his manuscripts he wrote, *"Jesu luva,"*[2] which is Latin for "Jesus, help!" I thank Andrew Peterson for pointing this out. I have made it my cry for *Questions of the Heart*. May it become your prayer as you share the Good News of Jesus Christ with your friends.

Jesu luva!
Kevin Thumpston

1. Ranald Macaulay and Jerram Barrs, *Being Human: The Nature of Spiritual Experience* (Downers Grove: InterVarsity Press, 1978), 82.
2. Andrew Peterson, *Adorning the Dark: Thoughts on Community, Calling and the Mystery of Making* (Nashville: B&H Publishing Group, 2019), 8.

AS IF I WAS HUMAN

For the glory of God is a human being fully alive; and
the life of man consists in beholding God.
> —Irenaeus of Lyons, *Against Heresies*

When our church plant was about a year old, one late
afternoon I had gathered the leaders together for a
strategic planning meeting. You know how hard it is to
get everyone together for these types of meetings, so I
was pumped the whole team was available. As I was
about to start, the front door swung open and in came
John, a slender spectacled young man with unkempt
black hair. He hobbled in on a crutch to relieve the pain
in his leg, which was a bloody mess. He'd been hit by
a car.

Without looking up he asked, "Excuse me, could I
speak with someone?"

I breathed a deep sigh and flippantly cast a glance

toward the planning team as if to say, "Give me a minute to deal with this interruption, so we can get back to the important business of the church."

As John and I entered my office, I asked him, "What can I do for you? Do you want some money or some food?"

He meekly expressed the question of his heart, "I don't want a handout. I don't want any food or money. Could you just speak to me as if I was a human?"

His question grabbed my heart that day and has never let me go!

My understanding of how to accomplish the important business of the church and how to lovingly share the Gospel with those in my life  *as if they were human* has become one and the same. John's identity was shaped by lies, by those who had hurt him, by his own addictions, and by the sin that mastered him. When John limped into my life he was the walking dead, but through the Gospel he found new life and a new identity in Christ. The details of John's story may be unique, but his longing to find his identity is something we all deeply desire, whether we know it or not.

For most of my Christian life, sharing the Gospel has consisted of asking people diagnostic questions I wanted them to answer. I then followed up with a series of biblical reasons why they should answer my questions the way I wanted.

This may seem acceptable to do with acquaintances, but to treat friends, family, co-workers and neighbors like this is awkward and rude. It also seems unseasoned in our day and age to ask someone about their eternal destiny out of the blue.

I do believe there is a time and place for all types of evangelistic approaches. I commend my fellow believers in doing the work of evangelism, as well as the groups that have trained up thousands of believers to share their faith with such means. I mention confrontational methods of evangelism only because I have a hard time consistently using them with people I do life with from day to day. To be honest, for many years I settled for not doing anything at all because it didn't seem to fit the relationship. And trust me, I have been trained well with extensive evangelistic tools.

When I first became a Christian at the University of South Carolina (USC), the radical change in my life was so obvious that people couldn't help but ask me what had happened. This made sharing my faith easy. I was so  excited to tell people. You couldn't shut me up. I told all my fraternity brothers at the keg parties, my fellow waiters in the restaurant, and my neighbors at the mailbox. I shared my new-found faith with my family, friends, and anyone else who would listen.

As I grew in my faith, an emotional testimony didn't seem to be substantive enough, so I began my journey into learning more methodical ways of evangelism. Campus Crusade taught me to share the Four Spiritual Laws with fellow college students. After college, I used the Wordless Book/ Bracelets by Child Evangelism Fellowship with kids in government housing. As a youth pastor, I shared the Romans Road and One Verse Evangelism by The Navigators.

I became a trainer for Evangelism Explosion. At Covenant Theological Seminary, I studied apologetics with Jerram Barrs, focusing on relationship evangelism. As a church planter, I sought to develop missional communities. Most recently, I used the Near and Far Approach and Prayer Walks to bless my neighbors. Even with all this training, I still wrestle with sharing the Gospel in a consistent manner with those closest to me.

Since culture and people change, we invent new ways to sin and what seems like novel ways to redefine our core identity. Evangelism seems like a moving target in this environment with these conditions. Years ago in New York, Pastor Tim Keller discovered that morality-based evangelism wasn't as effective with the urban-enlightened, those who were not driven by being good but by being free, so he pivoted toward the freedom found in the Gospel. If we look deep into the Gospel and the heart of man, we see that evangelism could take on countless approaches, because the Gospel applies to every human need.

As Christians, those under the authority of Scripture, we know that there is only one true Gospel, so the question is not, "What Gospel are we to share?"

"The gospel is called the 'good news' because it addresses the most serious problem that you and I have as human beings, and that problem is simply this: God is holy and He is just, and I'm not. And at the end of my life, I'm going to stand before a just and holy God, and I'll be judged. And I'll be judged either on the basis of my own righteousness—or lack of it—or the righteousness of another. The good news of the gospel is that Jesus lived a life of perfect righteousness, of perfect obedience to God, not for His own well being but for His people. He has done for me what I couldn't possibly do for myself. But not only has He lived that life of perfect obedience, He offered Himself as a perfect sacrifice to satisfy the justice and the righteousness of God." (R.C. Sproul)

The question is actually, "How are we to share the Gospel to this generation?"

Author Sam Chan elaborates:

In the Bible, there is no single method of communicating the gospel, instead there is a variety of methods. In the New Testament alone, we find

Parables by Jesus

Songs

Creeds

Letters to churches

One-on-one conversations

Sermons in formal worship gatherings

Discussion meetings

Public speeches

Apocalyptic literature

Miracles

Unfortunately, well-meaning Christians often get stuck on one particular method and end up believing it is the only or best method. Usually this is the method that we have become an expert in. Or it is the method that was effective in our own conversion. Or it is the method that distinguishes our tradition or denomination from others.[1]

Strategically, we should not settle for one method but store up as many evangelistic models as possible, so we can be ready to share the Gospel in any situation. Author Samuel Wells has an interesting perspective on ethics that I think applies to evangelism. He proposes that Christian ethics is a lot like improvisation. He writes, "Christian ethics and theatrical improvisation are both about years of steeping in a tradition so that the body is so soaked in practices and perceptions that it trusts itself in community to do the obvious thing."[2]

This shouldn't be mistaken with situational ethics, where the situation dictates the ethic. Wells suggests we should have a deep understanding of Scripture which enables us to apply the truth of God to any situation. Each and every morning, we won't know what situation we will find ourselves in or who we may encounter, so we must steep ourselves in the Scriptures, prayer, and as many useful evangelistic models to be ready to share with our friends.

Warren Buffet's right-hand man, Charlie Munger, was a master at financial decision-making. He developed a latticework of mental models[3] to immediately pull from to answer the plethora of economic questions that came

his way. We would be wise to develop a latticework of evangelistic models to help answer the questions of our friends' hearts.

With this in mind, I would like to offer you another model for sharing your faith, especially with those whom you have an ongoing relationship. I call it *Questions of the Heart*.

---

1. Sam Chan, *Evangelism in A Skeptical World: How to Make the Unbelievable News about Jesus more Believable* (Grand Rapids: Zondervan Academic, 2018), 16–17.
2. Samuel Wells, *Improvisation: The Drama of Christian Ethics* (Grand Rapids: Brazos Press, 2004), 17.
3. Andrew McVagh, "Charlie Munger's System Of Mental Models: How To Think Your Way To Success," My Mental Models, August 7, 2018, https://www.mymentalmodels.info/charlie-munger-mental-models/.

THREE FACTORS

OUR CULTURE'S DEEPENING IDENTITY CRISIS

THE DEMAND FOR SELF-DISCOVERY

THE UNIQUE CRY OF EACH INDIVIDUAL HEART

Crisis
An incipient moment of danger, a time when things start to go awry, a perilous situation when one should be especially wary.

Many factors played a role in the development of *Questions of the Heart*. What follows are a few of the most significant ones.

Identity Crisis

A simple glance at our Tilt-A-World reveals that we are in a national identity crisis. Shayne Looper of huffpost.com writes:

> America is lost. She doesn't know where she is or in which direction she should be moving. There are people on the left, shouting to her to come their way and people on the right, doing the same. Worse than not knowing where she is, America no longer knows who she is.[1]

This generation is not unique in regard to misplaced identity, but this generation is more vocal about it and has more outlets to do so than previous generations. With a multitude of social media profiles, online influencers, and no lack of etched body ink, this generation is confronted with the same question as all generations, "Who am I?" In a piece in *The Atlantic*, Chris Weller points out:

> For some, that choice is liberating: It's a chance to start from scratch. For others, the sheer volume of options can be paralyzing. In either case, modernity compels us to declare our identity with conviction, whether we've found it or not.[2]

It feels a bit like the book of Judges to me, where the next generation invents new ways to define themselves and conjures up more creative ways to sin. The reality is that each generation has to pick up the pieces the previous generation left for them. Sorry kids! We are leaving you in a full-blown identity crisis—gender confusion, the call-out movement, social media addiction, racial wars, the opioid epidemic, sex-trafficking, the withdrawal from marriage and the de-humanization of the unborn. These are just a sampling of the devastating fallout of this generation's crisis of identity. We have not simply bucked at a biblical worldview but redefined what it means to be human all together. Out of fear, we prepared the road for our children, rather than our children for the road.

We have coddled the newest generation Gen Z by believing "three Great Untruths that seem to have spread widely in recent years:

The Untruth of Fragility: What doesn't kill you makes you weaker.
The Untruth of Emotional Reasoning: Always trust your feelings.
The Untruth of Us Versus Them: Life is a battle between good people and evil people."[3]

Along with the negative effects of our coddling, Gen Z must face disruption and difficult crises of their own. The 2018 study by XYZ University explains:

Of course, Gen Z is known for being tech savvy, but more than technology, the members of this generation have been shaped by the crises they were born into: the rise of school shootings, climate change, terrorism and the Great Recession.

These dark events have undoubtedly made this generation more cautious and pragmatic, but they have also provided this generation with the inspiration to change the world....

In many ways, it's symbolic that Generation Z is named after the last letter in the alphabet because their arrival marks the end of clearly defined roles, traditions, and experiences. After all, Generation Z is coming of age on the heels of what has been referred to as the most disruptive decade of the last century. America has become an increasingly changing and complex place.[4]

A few findings of this new disrupted generation are: a concept of family that is more diverse than ever before; a hacker, hero and builder mentality due to corruption; a matrix reality, where everything physical, from people to places to pennies, has a digital equivalent; a fierce competitive drive with an entrepreneurial hunger to curate/create; and a new community with lessened racial stigma. Just like preceding generations, there are many challenges, but there are also huge opportunities to share the Gospel and transform lives.

Only through the Gospel can this and every generation discover who God truly is and who they are in light of him. The Gospel begins by making the great distinction of humanity over the rest of creation in that we, man and woman alike, are created in the image of God. The One who made us and the One who upholds us has put his imprint on us. His identity is stamped into the very fabric of our being: heart, mind, body and soul. This reality will never change, but our sin has distorted this reality and made us into glorious ruins. Every aspect of our being is now soiled with rebellion. Only through the life, death, and resurrection of Christ can our rebellion be conquered and our identity crisis be redeemed.

Self-Discovery

Another feature passed down to our present generation is a mistrust of authoritative directives due to the abuse of power they have witnessed and experienced. Millennials put on the lenses of skepticism and mistrust, and nobody has taken them off. Kipp Jarecke-Cheng writes:

> For media- and tech-savvy Millennials, the erosion of trust has become so severe that only 2 out of 10 major institutions—the military and the scientific community —garnered a majority of positive support, according to a poll of young people conducted by Harvard University's Institute of Politics. In the same poll, 88% of Millennials said they "only sometimes" or "never" trust the press and 86% of Millennials said they distrust Wall Street. Millennials were equally dubious of government, with 74% saying they "sometimes" or

"never" trust that the federal government will do the right thing.

When it comes to religion, Millennials' views have become markedly more negative over time, with 55% of Millennials surveyed by the Pew Research Center rating churches and other religious organizations as having a positive impact on the country compared to 73% of young people responding to the same question five years ago.[5]

Due to this menagerie of mistrust, people want to find answers for themselves and not simply be told what to believe. Therefore, we must make room for listening, conversation, and patience. Our present generations are also consumed by what has been termed "the Quantified Self"[6] which digitally tracks one's behavior—every step, sleep pattern, diaper change, calorie consumption, and purchase, but it is at a loss in measuring one's true identity.

Self-discovery and behavioral quantification pursued for self-centered therapeutic reasons only leads to more confusion. Those who are in Christ are called to help our friends measure their identity with the only true scale—the Gospel—but we must do it through self-discovery. Therefore, we must flip our approach from asking questions we want this generation to answer to listening for the questions of their hearts and helping them find their answers in Christ.

Rather than backing our friends into a decision corner, we can sit down with them and let the questions of their heart lead the conversation. We can help them discover a biblical worldview where Christ speaks into their fallen and sinful humanity. Our friends need to trip over the truth rather than be indoctrinated.

In Chip and Dan Heath's insightful book *The Power of Moments*, they summarize the findings of Dr. Kamal Kar in a study on the deadly effects of open defecation in Bangladesh. Kar demonstrates the power of self-discovery over dictating a solution. After the failure of systematically placing latrines in the communities, Kar walked the villagers through the process of self-discovery with great results.

Kar said that the villagers will often tell him:

> This is a truth which nobody wanted to discuss. We're always pushing it under the carpet—and then it was brought out in public and into the daylight.... Now there's no way out. The naked truth is out. They didn't really "see" the truth until they were made to trip over it. Tripping over the truth is an insight that packs an emotional wallop. When you have a sudden realization, one that you didn't see coming, and one that you know viscerally is right, you've tripped over the truth. It's a defining moment that in an instant can change the way you see the world.[7]

This generation needs to trip over their own mess to come to grips with the truth and to own their need for Jesus. As people discover biblical solutions for their immediate challenges and crises, we can trust the Holy Spirit to lead them deeper toward the eternal crisis of their heart and to find new life in Christ. Instead of forcing the issue, we get to witness the Holy Spirit supernaturally open the eyes and hearts of our friends.

Unique Heart Cry

There is only One True Gospel, but the questions of the heart are not answered by a one-size-fits all rote evangelistic method. Instead of using our favorite lure, we should find out what our friends are hungry for. The present need of their heart is the sweet spot and the momentary place of teachability. We each have our own unique journey that God has set us on, filled with peaks and valleys. It's usually in the desert times where God gets our attention. In *Ravished by Beauty*, Beldan Lane explains the nature of the desert and its spiritual significance:

> Oddly enough, the desert is the best place to study water. Its landscape is defined by the memory of rain, etched into the land at every turn. Its surface is carved into canyons, arroyos, cañoncitos, ravines, narrows, washes, and chasms. The anatomy of [the] place has no other profession but the moving of water. A remembrance of flow lingers in the shadow of every rock. This is how the desert knows water—achingly, desperately, with a passion bordering on dread. It's the only way we ever know God as well.[8]

Even as glorious ruins, there is a remembrance of our true identity etched in the contours of our heart. Pascal affirms:

What else does this craving, and this helplessness, proclaim but that there was once in man a true happiness, of which all that now remains is the empty print and trace? This he tries in vain to fill with everything around him, seeking in things that are not there the help he cannot find in those that are, though none can help, since this infinite abyss can be filled only with an infinite and immutable object; in other words by God himself.[9]

In a culture of "no one understands me," we must take the time to let our friends explain. We must meet them in the ache and desperation. The questions of the heart for someone licking the wounds of a broken relationship is much different from the anxiety of someone presenting their PhD dissertation or fighting addiction. Walking with our friends through these critical moments of life with Gospel truth is a way to truly bless them and to introduce them to our Lord and Savior, Jesus Christ.

Our identity is always being challenged away from faith by the pride of ignorance and arrogance. We must listen for our friends' governing disposition and how their identity is being uniquely challenged before applying the balm of the Gospel. We must be wary of our assumptions. Our assumptions about our friends can cause us to answer the questions we think they need answering, instead of the actual pressing issues of their heart. Author Todd Henry notes the two sides of our assumptions:

Jeff Hawkins in his book *On Intelligence* contends that our minds function by constantly predicting what will happen next and then comparing these predictions with what we actually experience. In doing so we develop patterns that make our future predictions more accurate, a library of experiences against which we can validate new information. This allows us to make many decisions in our life quickly, often based upon hunches and with very little information. While this capacity is helpful in allowing us to assimilate new information and experiences quickly and usefully, it can also mire us in mental ruts that prevent us from seeing opportunities.... Instead, we see only the world through the lens of our assumptions, whether they're true or false.[10]

Jesus was a master listener and chose his questions carefully, aiming at the heart. In the gospel records, he asked 307 questions.[11] As Jesus interacted with people, Scripture says that he knew what was in their hearts and minds (Matt. 12:18, 25; Mark 2:8; Luke 6:8, 11:17, 16,15; John 2:25). Granted Jesus is God and knows all things, but he also grew in wisdom and stature before God and man (Luke 2:52). Let's not rule out that Jesus knew their hearts and minds from the study of Scripture and by carefully watching and listening to people. Since we are not omniscient, we will do well to practice the latter to avoid wrong assumptions. Jesus Christ listened and spoke to the inmost place of every heart and dealt with every aspect of life. He wasn't just a listening ear, but the very answer they were looking for. He was and is the answer to every question of the heart

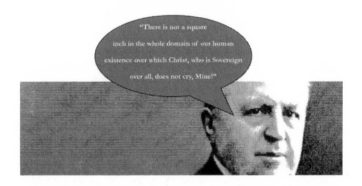

Abraham Kuyper summarized it well: "There is not a square inch in the whole domain of our human existence over which Christ, who is Sovereign over all, does not cry, Mine!"[12]

---

1. Shayne Looper, "America is Suffering An Identity Crisis," Huffpost.com, January 18, 2018, https://www.huffpost.com/entry/america-is-suffering-an-i_b_14150438.

2. Chris Weller, "The Identity Crisis Under the Ink," theatlantic.com, November 25, 2014, https://www.theatlantic.com/health/archive/2014/11/the-identity-crisis-under-the-ink/382785/.

3. Greg Lukianoff and Jonathan Haidt, *The Coddling of The American Mind: How Good Intentions and Bad Ideas are Setting Up A Generation For Failure* (New York: Penguin Press, 2018), 4.

4. Sarah Sladek and Josh Miller, "Ready Or Not Here Comes Z," January 2019, https:// www.xyzuniversity.com/wp-content/uploads/2018/08/Ready-or-Not-Here-Comes-Z-Final.pdf.

5. Kipp Jarecke-Cheng, "Millennials And The Age Of Distrust", mediapost.com, February 24, 2017, https://www.mediapost.com/publications/article/295856/millennials-and-the-age-of-distrust.html.

6. Gary Wolf, "The Quantified Self," ted.com, June 2010, https://www.ted.com/talks/gary_wolf_the_quantified_self   ? language=en.

7. Chip and Dan Heath, *The Power of Moments: Why Certain Experiences Have Extraordinary Impact* (New York: Simon & Schuster), 102–103.

8. Belden C. Lane, *Ravished by Beauty: The Surprising Legacy of Reformed Spirituality* (Oxford: Oxford Press, 2011), 1–2.

9. Blaise Pascal, *Pensées*, (New York; Penguin Books, 1966), 75.

10. Todd Henry, *The Accidental Creative: How to Be Brilliant at a Moment's Notice* (New York, Penguin Group, 2013), 71–72.

11. Martin B. Copenhaver, *Jesus is the Question: The 307 Questions Jesus Asked and the 3 He Answered* (Nashville: Abingdon Press, 2014), 16.

12. Abraham Kuyper, *A Centennial Reader*, ed. James D. Bratt (Grand Rapids: W.B. Eerdmans; Carlisle: Paternoster Press, 1998), 488.

LEAN IN, LISTEN FOR, AND LOVE WELL
A BIBLICAL MODEL

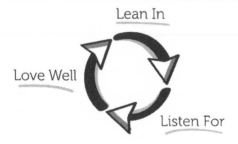

The Apostle Paul urges believers to lean in, listen for, and love well. Let's see what he says in the book of Colossians. Paul writes:

> *Continue steadfastly in prayer, being watchful in it with thanksgiving. At the same time, pray also for us, that God may*

open to us a door for the word, to declare the mystery of Christ, on account of which I am in prison— that I may make it clear, which is how I ought to speak. Walk in wisdom toward outsiders, making the best use of the time. Let your speech always be gracious, seasoned with salt, so that you may know how you ought to answer each person. Col. 4:2–6

Lean In: The Heart of God

First and foremost, we are to lean into the heart of our Sovereign Lord and King through prayer. Paul urges us to *"continue steadfastly in prayer and to be watchful in it."* We must lean into the Lord, the only one who changes hearts and applies the gospel by the Holy Spirit. J. I. Packer writes, "The prayer of a Christian is not an attempt to force God's hand, but a humble acknowledgement of helpless dependence... what we do every time we pray is to confess our own impotence and God's sovereignty."[1] Prayer is where we transition what we think about God and his mission to knowing him and making him known to others. Tim Keller puts it this way: "Conversation with God leads to an encounter with God.... Prayer turns theology into experience. Through it we sense his presence and receive his joy, his love, his peace, and confidence, and thereby we are changed in attitude, behavior, and character."[2]

In prayer, we entrust our friends to the greatest Friend of Sinners! Through prayer, Jesus invites us into a friendship. As his friends, Jesus reveals the desires of his heart in an even much greater degree than we share our heart and life with our friends. In their book *Engage*, authors John Smed and Justine Hwang write:

> We enjoy Jesus' friendship in prayer as we dialogue with him. Apart from prayer, friendship with Jesus can never begin or grow. In prayer with Jesus we grow rich in our friendship with him and rich in our friendship toward Others.... We live out his friendship as we intercede on behalf of others.[3]

Neal McGlohon, a leader of Cypress Project, challenged a group of us church planters with this question: "If God were to answer all your prayers from last week, how many people would enter the kingdom of God today?"

Jesus has also made us his ambassadors. Therefore, we must ask him how to be his earthly representatives and with whom we are to share the good news of his kingdom. We must pray with expectation that God will open the doors of the gospel, so that we can walk through them with confidence and humility. By faith, we know that "God's will" will be done and that he will empower us to humbly proclaim the gospel to those whom he is calling. We must take Jesus at his word. He said, *"Apart from me you can do nothing"* (John 15:5).

Did you know that the ascended Jesus spends his time interceding for us and for those whom we share the Gospel with? Paul writes, *"Christ Jesus is the one who died—more than that, who was raised—who is at the right hand of God, who indeed is interceding for us"* (Ro. 8:34).

Our prayers really matter. In Revelation 8, God says

that they are like thunder and lightning thrust upon the earth from heaven. John writes:

> *And another angel came and stood at the altar with a golden censer, and he was given much incense to offer with the prayers of all the saints on the golden altar before the throne, and the smoke of the incense, with the prayers of the saints, rose before God from the hand of the angel. Then the angel took the censer and filled it with fire from the altar and threw it on the earth, and there were peals of thunder, rumblings, flashes of lightning, and an earthquake.* Rev. 8:3–5

We must also lean into God's Word, so that we can know how and what we are to speak to those around us. God's Word is his infallible and inerrant communication with us. Through his Word and by his Spirit, God continues to make *"his appeal through us"* (2 Cor. 5:20). The Scriptures are ripe with how God engages people with identity challenges and crises. It tells God's redemptive story of how he rescues sinners and brings them back into fellowship with him. The Scriptures reveal our past, present, and future story. It gives us wisdom to glorify God and to enjoy him now and forevermore. His Word is not a dead ancient text, but *"is living and active, sharper than any two-edged sword, piercing to the division of soul and of spirit, of joints and of marrow, and discerning the thoughts and intentions of the heart"* (Heb. 4:12). His Word will never return void, and it will accomplish that which God purposes. Isaiah writes:

For as the rain and the snow come down from heaven and do not return there but water the earth, making it bring forth and sprout, giving seed to the sower and bread to the eater, so shall my word be that goes out from my mouth; it shall not return to me empty, but it shall accomplish that which I purpose, and shall succeed in the thing for which I sent it. Isa. 55:10–11

As we read, study, memorize, and meditate on Scripture and listen to the preached Word, we will become more proficient in applying the Word of God to the questions of our hearts and the hearts of our friends. Evangelism is about knowing God and his Word rather than memorizing an evangelistic methodology!

> Evangelism is about knowing God and his Word rather than memorizing an evangelistic methodology!

Lean In: The Heart of Our Friends

Instead of walking away from or avoiding the mess of our friends' lives, we are called to walk in wisdom toward outsiders.

Yes, you heard me. I said you should enter into the crisis of your friends' lives. It's a difficult saying, but remember Jesus left heaven and took on flesh to come after us. Scott Sauls encourages us in his book *Befriend*. He writes:

REAL FRIENDSHIP IS HARD. There are other, less real versions of friendship. The less real versions are "less" because they are less costly, less committed, less disruptive, less scary, less gritty, less gutsy, and less out-of-control than real friendship. But here's the rub: Less real versions of friendship are also less rich.[4]

Leaning in can be as simple as showing hospitality by inviting our friends into our life on our turf and demonstrating mercy by entering into their lives on their turf. To be honest, I can be a grump. I also get distracted sometimes, so people can wonder if I am excited or interested about being with them. A while back, a friend invited me to play golf with him and another guy. His friend's interest in me and kindness toward me had a lasting impression. I can't remember his friend's name, but I'll never forget he made me feel like I was the most important person in the world. I guess I don't remember his name because his attention was on me and not himself. May God help us to be kind and to put our friend's interests above our own. May our lives have a lasting impact on others, where our names don't really matter because all they remember is Jesus'.

However, there can be a danger in leaning in the wrong way. James White, a pastor in Cary, North Carolina, once warned me of the Savior-complex. He told me, "We are not responsible 'for' our friends' salvation, but we are responsible 'to' them." Leaning in doesn't mean we become their Savior, but we are responsible to be a true friend to them by pointing them to the Savior. We can trust Jesus to guide and uphold our friends through their crisis. I recommend bringing someone else with you in the rougher situations. There are reasons why Jesus sent the disciples out in twos: for encouragement, to model community, for accountability, and to deepen wisdom.

We all know the estrangement of being an outsider. We know how lonely it is and how desperate it feels to want to belong. C. S. Lewis wrote about the elusive longing for the Inner Ring, the desire to belong and to be on the inside:

> I believe that in all men's lives at certain periods, and in many men's lives at all periods between infancy and extreme old age, one of the most dominant elements is the desire to be inside the local Ring and the terror of being left outside.[5]

With the Gospel, we have the great privilege of inviting our friends and neighbors into the very presence of God, the only true Inner Ring. Through Christ, he has taken away the dividing line between us and our Holy God.

Paul adds that we should lean into our friends' lives with thanksgiving. I once did a sermon titled, "If Jesus came to Thanksgiving dinner, what would he give thanks for?" In my study, I looked through the gospels to see what Jesus gave thanks for. I was shocked at my findings, and how little the gospels recorded Jesus giving thanks. I limited my search to the main Greek word for "giving thanks." Here are five of the times Jesus gave thanks. He gave thanks at the tomb of Lazarus. He gave thanks at both the feedings of the multitudes. He gave thanks at the Passover meal with his disciples and again as he broke bread with Cleopas and his friend on the road to Emmaus.

I was humbled at what his thanksgiving revealed. At Lazarus' tomb, Jesus gave thanks that his Father always hears him and that the Father would grant faith to those listening. John writes:

> *And Jesus lifted up his eyes and said, "Father, I thank you that you have heard me. I knew that you always hear me, but I said this on account of the people standing around, that they may believe that you sent me.* John 11:41–42

Jesus also gave thanks as an act of faith. At each of the feedings, he gave thanks before the Father did the miracle of multiplying the fish and the loaves of bread. That struck me as odd, because I usually give thanks looking at a full plate of food or after God answers one of my prayers, not beforehand. Jesus' thanksgiving revealed that he trusted the Father before his prayers were answered. Matthew writes:

> *Then he ordered the crowds to sit down on the grass, and taking the five loaves and the two fish, he looked up to heaven and said a blessing. Then he broke the loaves and gave them to the disciples, and the disciples gave them to the crowds.* Matt. 14:19

At the Passover with his disciples and breaking bread with the two men from the Emmaus Road, Jesus gave thanks not in response to receiving a personal benefit to himself but to the opportunity of sacrificially dying for those under his care. We read:

> *Now as they were eating, Jesus took bread, and after blessing it broke it and gave it to the disciples, and said, "Take, eat; this is my body." And he took a cup, and when he had given thanks he gave it to them, saying, "Drink of it, all of you, for this is my blood of the covenant, which is poured out for many for the forgiveness of sins.* Matt. 26:26–28

> *When he was at table with them, he took the bread and blessed and broke it and gave it to them. And their eyes were opened, and they recognized him. And he vanished from their sight. They said to each other, "Did not our hearts burn within us while he talked to us on the road, while he opened to us the Scriptures?"* Luke 24:30–32

May Jesus' example of giving thanks shape how we share our faith. We can have confidence that our Father always hears us and will draw those listening to himself. May we thankfully share the Gospel knowing that God will do immeasurably more than all we ask or think. And may we sacrificially demonstrate the love of Jesus to our friends. In thanksgiving, sharing our faith becomes an adventure and blessing rather than a burden.

What a privilege it is that God would send us to go and fetch his sons and daughters—to tell them of their true identity and bring them home.

One of the best ways of redeeming our time as Christians is to invite people into a relationship with Christ —to share with them the good news of the life, death and resurrection of Christ.

> *What a privilege it is that God would send us to go and fetch his sons and daughters — to tell them of their true identity and bring them home.*

However, most days we treat evangelism like cleaning the house or washing the car. We know we ought to do it, but it never quite makes our priority list. We need to start thinking of it as one of the best uses of our time, wisely applying the truth of God to the questions of the heart.

I love that Paul says to *"walk in wisdom,"* which infers that the way we conduct ourselves, the way we practically live out our faith, the way we lean into the lives of others is a catalyst for gospel curiosity. Wisdom can take on many shapes: an honest work ethic, raising kids with joy, showing compassion to the least of them, treating all people with respect, helping out a stranger or showing grace when wronged. Our conduct is huge when it comes to sharing our faith!

Paul gave thanks for Philemon and exhorted him to share his faith by showing Onesimus mercy:

> *I thank my God always when I remember you in my prayers, because I hear of your love and of the faith that you have toward the Lord Jesus and for all the saints, and I pray that the sharing of your faith may become effective for the full knowledge of every good thing that is in us for the sake of Christ. For I have derived much joy and comfort from your love, my brother, because the hearts of the saints have been*

*refreshed through you.... So if you consider me your partner,
receive him as you would receive me.* Phile. 4–7, 17

I need to ask myself if I treat all people—perhaps
those I have in mind with *Questions of the Heart*—with
respect, mercy, and love.

Sometimes people need more
than an explanation of love. They
need to see love before they can
understand it. Donald Miller, author
of *Blue Like Jazz*, explains the impor-
tance of seeing someone love
something:

> I never liked jazz music because jazz music doesn't
> resolve. But I was outside the Bagdad Theater in
> Portland one night when I saw a man playing the
> saxophone. I stood there for fifteen minutes, and he
> never opened his eyes. After that I liked jazz music.
> Sometimes you have to watch somebody love
> something before you can love it yourself. It is as if
> they are showing you the way. I used to not like God
> because God didn't resolve. But that was before any of
> this happened.[6]

Listen For: Being Watchful

As we lean into the heart of God and to the heart of our
friends, we must listen—*be watchful*—for their crisis of
identity. In Paul Miller's book, *Love Walked Among Us*,
and in the companion *Person of Jesus* study, he points out

that Jesus was always "Looking."[7] "On nearly forty different occasions in the gospels, Jesus either looks at people, tells others to look, or teaches about looking."[8] As Jesus walked on the earth, he looked for the opportunities his Father had prepared for him. He listened for their heart questions and offered the truth of the Gospel. John writes:

> *As he passed by, he saw a man blind from birth. And his disciples asked him, "Rabbi, who sinned, this man or his parents, that he was born blind?" Jesus answered, "It was not that this man sinned, or his parents, but that the works of God might be displayed in him."* John 9:1–3

As friends of Jesus, the Father has called us to do the same type of looking for opportunities. We must be watchful for these opportunities! Author Mike Mason writes, "We are to practice the presence of people." We are to have our eyes and ears open in the culture we live in, to understand the idols of our community and to listen for the questions of our friends' hearts.

Mason continues:

> The practice of the presence of people is not some spectator sport that can be done from the sidelines. We're not talking about people-watching, but about love. Love requires getting mixed up with people. We're going to spend a lot of our lives mixed up anyway. Why not do it together?[9]

In *Telling the Truth*, Frederick Buechner encourages us to also listen to the silence. He writes:

> Words are what he chiefly has to use but remembering always that the silence that his words frame—the silence that his words are born out of and that his words break and that his words are swallowed up by—may well convey the mystery of truth better than the words themselves.[10]

We must listen for the silence that our friends live in —the emptiness of life, the isolation apart from God and allow them to experience the silence for themselves. For many, it's the first time in their lives. It is our nature to add more blah, blah, blah rather than invite silence into our friends' lives, so they can hear, *"Be still and know that I am God"* (Ps. 46:10). A good friend sits and listens in the silence before uttering a single word.

Listen For: Making it Clear

Paul wanted to uniquely answer each person clearly with the gospel. When a person's identity is being challenged or in crisis, he or she is focused on that one issue. We need to listen for this focal point of need, so that we can apply the Gospel clearly to bring it into the light. Our lives are most vulnerable during our dark moments where we can't find a way out and everything is clouded by the crisis of identity.

Paul asked for prayer that he could speak forth the brilliance of the Gospel into the darkness of those around him. When Paul asked for that opportunity, he was in prison, and he still made it a priority to share the Gospel. (What excuses are you making for not sharing your faith today?) As we hear the crisis of identity in those around us, we are called to take the opportunity to clearly share the Gospel and its application.

In listening for the crisis of identity, we must look through the common lens of the *imago Dei*, the biblical doctrine that all people are created in the image of God. Our identity has been sculpted and defined by God. We have capacities to reason, to relate, and to rule. Due to sin, we have all sought to define ourselves and give ourselves purpose and value in everything but God. Sin distorts the way we think, the way we relate with others and the way we engage the world. In trying to sort through the complexity of identity, we fall prey to defining ourselves with lesser secondary, earthly identities, rather than the *imago Dei*.

Amin Maalouf, a Lebanese Christian who lived in France for twenty-two years, goes into great length about the complexity and sometimes devastating effects of secondary identity allegiances. He writes:

> Identity can't be compartmentalized. You can't divide it up into halves or thirds or any other separate segments. I haven't got several identities. I've just one, made up of many components in a mixture that is unique to me, just as other people's identity is unique to them as individuals. Each individual identity is made up of a number of elements, and these are clearly not restricted to the particulars set down in official

records. Of course, for the great majority these factors include allegiance to a religious tradition—sometimes two; to a profession, and institution, or a particular social milieu. But the list is much longer than that; it is virtually unlimited.... One could find dozens of other examples to show how complex is the mechanism of identity: a complexity sometimes benign, but sometimes tragic.[11]

He wrestles with how allegiances to secondary identities fuel wars and atrocities all in the name of "identity." We create enemies of anyone who is identified as "other" than us. In Scripture, we see that we must go deeper than earthly identities as a common denominator of mankind. We must go back to creation with the *imago Dei*, and we must acknowledge our common depravity from the Fall (Genesis 3) and our ongoing sin nature to democratize man's need for one true identity. Once we see our common need, by grace through faith, we begin to see that there is only one who can redeem us and offer us our true identity, namely Jesus Christ. Paul writes, *"For there is no distinction: for all have sinned and fall short of the glory of God, and are justified by his grace as a gift, through the redemption that is in Christ Jesus"* (Ro. 3:22–24).

The culprit of our misplaced identity is a prideful, two-faced rebellion of ignorance and arrogance. Faith is threatened constantly by the postures of ignorance and arrogance, which swing us into an identity crisis, where we exchange the truth of God for a lie.

By faith, we fight against the pride of ignorance and

arrogance. By faith, our lives are realigned to God's will. By faith, our identity is redeemed. According to Scripture, we live out our true identity by faith as learners, worshipers, beloved, neighbors, culturemakers, and servants. In the pride of ignorance, we become fools, idolaters, orphans, loners, consumers, and sloths. In the pride of arrogance, we become experts, cynics, entitled, politicians, whiners, and narcissists. We must listen for our friends' predominant posture toward God and the specific aspect of their identity being challenged or in crisis.

————

In his book *God & Tattoos*, Allan Dayhoff tells the story of meeting and listening to his waitress at The Burger Joint. She was a naturally beautiful woman in her mid-thirties. He asks her about the thoughtful tattoo that draped over her shoulder. As you will see, her identity has been challenged leaving her and her daughter as a loner and orphan. Dayhoff writes:

> I said, "I like your tattoo," as I looked at its direction. She cast her eyes over to it and said, "Yeah, it's me and the moon. Like your burger?" She asked. "Yes, and could you roll me to my car please?" I answered. I waited, and the pause paid off, as she continued, "I got divorced this year and it's just me and my five-year-old daughter. We are making it, but it's been hard and

dark. But even when it's dark, sometimes the moon keeps you company right? My daughter has nightmares about daddy never coming back again." I waited again, not moving a muscle, perhaps like a hunter waiting for a prize elk to come out of the brush. The pause seemed to allow her heart to speak. "Loneliness comes in the middle of the night sometimes, when I can't sleep. I found that the moon became a reminder that there is hope, and while some things change, others stay the same. The moon and me, we became good friends.... She hugged me and she looked into my eyes for a moment before I left as though she was happy to be understood.[12]

Everyone longs to be listened to and understood—from the waitress at The Burger Joint, to the newly married couple next door, to a brother or sister, to the elderly gentleman in the nursing home.

Love Well: Always Be Gracious

In Colossians 4:6, Paul writes, *"Let your speech always be gracious, seasoned with salt, so that you may know how you ought to answer each person."*

When we do speak, we must make sure our speech is gracious, not condemning or belittling. Gracious speech is always loving speech. This is a tall order when we enter into the lives of others. It is hard to love well with our own pride of blame-shifting, entitlement, manipulation, sloth, and narcissism. Loving well means we're guarding our own hearts, lifting the eyes of the lowly to see hope, and humbling the high and mighty to see their need.

As we walk in love with our friends, we must remember the dark path God has brought us through so we can enter into relationships with much grace knowing no one deserves God's favor. We also know the journey can be a long one, so we take the time to love them well in word and deed through the ups and downs, applying the Gospel along the way.

We work on being gracious because we know repentance and sanctification are progressive. They take time. We must linger in the tattered pages of our friends' story before we can expect to open the pages of the audacious story of the Gospel.

Mike Cosper notes:

At the heart of our faith is the bold claim that in a world full of stories, with world's worth of heroes, villains, comedies, tragedies, twists of fate, and surprise endings, there is really only one story. One grand narrative subsumes and encompasses all the other comings and goings of every creature—real or fictitious—on the earth.[13]

> "For the love of Christ controls us... Therefore, if anyone is in Christ, he is a new creation. The old has passed away; behold, the new has come. All this is from God, who through Christ reconciled us to himself and gave us the ministry of reconciliation; that is, in Christ God was reconciling the world to himself, not counting their trespasses against them, and entrusting to us the message of reconciliation. Therefore, we are ambassadors for Christ, God making his appeal through us. We implore you on behalf of Christ, be reconciled to God. For our sake he made him to be sin who knew no sin, so that in him we might become the righteousness of God.
>
> (2 Corinthians 5:14a,17- 21)

Love Well: Seasoned with Salt

Salt is a preservative and a flavor enhancer; therefore, sharing our faith should have a lasting influence and enhance the life of our friends. It doesn't end after a conversation. The gospel calls us to share the message and our lives as well. Paul states this wonderfully: *"So, being affectionately desirous of you, we were ready to share with you not only the gospel of God but also our own selves, because you had become very dear to us."* (1 Thess. 2:8).

The Gospel flourishes from the seed of faith into a new identity, then a new life, and it ultimately resides in a new family. Sharing our faith is not a quick fix, but an ongoing relationship. Bob Goff used to want to fix people, but now he just wants to be with them. In *Love Does*, he explains how a Young Life leader taught him this kind of love when he decided to drop out of school to find himself in the mountains. Randy had just gotten married, but grabbed his pack and joined him on the adventure (Of course Randy let his wife know). Goff writes:

> Randy had been with me, and I could tell that he was "with me" in spirit as much as with his presence. He was committed to me and he believed in me. I wasn't a project; I was his friend.... I learned that faith isn't about knowing all of the right stuff or obeying a list of rules. It's something more, something more costly because it involves being present and making a sacrifice. Perhaps that's why Jesus is sometimes called Immanuel—"God with us." I think that's what God

had in mind, for Jesus to be present, to just be with us. It's also what He has in mind for us when it comes to other people.[14]

Lasting evangelism and discipleship finds its home in a loving relationship. The gospel isn't just about getting individuals saved. It's about knitting the hearts of individuals together in Christ. When we share the gospel and our lives with each other, we become family —brothers and sisters used by God to build each other up. We are called to each other, for each other. Paul Miller captures succinctly what this kind of love looks like in his book *A Loving Life*. Love is "love without an exit strategy."[15]

Sometimes it's the unlikely people in our lives that have the greatest impact on our faith. Check out who Charles Spurgeon learned his theology from.

———

Mary King was the stout and sturdy cook at Newmarket Academy in Cambridge, England, when a young teenager named Charles Haddon Spurgeon enrolled in the fall of 1849. Over the next two years "Cook," as the students affectionately called her, would feed the boy far more than food. In his autobiography Spurgeon recounts:

> She was a good old soul [and] liked something very
> sweet indeed, good strong Calvinistic doctrine. Many a
> time we have gone over the covenant of grace together,
> and talked of the personal election of the saints, their
> union to Christ, their final perseverance, and what vital
> godliness meant; and I do believe I learnt more from
> her than I should have learned from any six doctors of
> divinity of the sort we have nowadays.[16]

While her handle on Scripture was impressive, King didn't live and move and have her being in the realm of ideas alone. She was a woman of vital godliness, one who "lived strongly" as well as "fed strongly." As Spurgeon reflected, "There are some Christian people who taste, and see, and enjoy religion in their own souls, and who get at a deeper knowledge of it than books can ever give them, though they should search all their days." King, he said, was one of those people. The Prince of Preachers never forgot King and the formative role she'd played in his life. "A cook taught me theology!" he would often say.

———

Hopefully, *Questions of the Heart* will help you to lean in, listen for, and love well your friends, family, neighbors and coworkers toward a true identity in Christ. Remember *Questions of the Heart* is not only for our non-Christian friends but also for Christian friends. Everyone's identity gets challenged almost every day. We need to be reminded to live by faith, realigning our identity continuously back to the Author and Perfecter of our faith—Jesus Christ.

The crazy thing about *Questions of the Heart* is that it really isn't about the questions we are asking, but the urgent questions our friends are asking. We get the great honor of helping them answer the questions of their heart through Scripture and walk alongside them for the long haul.

Jesus Christ truly is the answer to all their questions.

> "For all the promises of God find their Yes in him [Christ]. That is why it is through him that we utter our Amen to God for his glory."
> (2 Corinthians 1:20)

1. J. I. Packer, *Evangelism & The Sovereignty of God* (Downers Grove: Intervarsity Press, 1991), 11–12.

2. Timothy Keller, *Prayer: Experiencing Awe and Intimacy with God* (New York: Dutton, 2014), 80.

3. John Smed and Justine Hwang, *Engage: The Conversation with God, with Believers, with Seekers* (Vancouver: Prayer Current, 2016), 8.

4. Scott Sauls, *Befriend: Create Belonging in an Age Of Judgment, Isolation, And Fear* (Carol Stream: Tyndale House Publishers, Inc., 2016), 1.

5. C. S. Lewis, "The Inner Ring" a memorial Lecture at King's College, University of London, in 1944, https://www.lewissociety.org/innerring/.

6. Donald Miller, *Blue Like Jazz: Movie Edition: Nonreligious Thoughts on Christian Spirituality* (Nashville: Thomas Nelson; Limited, Media Tie In, Reprint edition, 2012), 7.

7. Paul Miller, *Love Walked Among Us: Learning to Love Like Jesus* (Colorado Springs: Navpress, 2001), 23–38.

8. Paul Miller, *The Person of Jesus Study: An Interactive Bible Study* (Leader's Manual) (Telford: WWW.SeeJesus.net, 2002), 15–30.

9. Mike Mason, *Practicing the Presence of People: How We Learn to Love* (Colorado Springs: Waterbrook Press, 1999), 13.

10. Frederick Buechner, *Telling the Truth: The Gospel as Tragedy, Comedy, and Fairy Tale* (New York: Harper One, 1977), 26.

11. Amin Maalouf, *In the Name of Identity: Violence and the Need to Belong* (New York: Arcade Publishing, 2012), 2, 10, 14.

12. Allan Dayhoff, *God & Tattoos: Why Are People Writing on Themselves?* (Morrisville: Lulu Publishing, 2016), 27–28.

13. Mike Cosper, *The Stories We Tell: How TV and Movies Long for and Echo the Truth* (Wheaton: Crossway, 2014), 28–29.

14. Bob Goff, *Love Does: Discover a Secretly Incredible Life in an Ordinary World* (Nashville: Thomas Nelson, 2012), 8–9.

15. Paul E. Miller, *A Loving Life: In a World of Broken Relationships* (Wheaton: Crossway, 2014), 24.

16. Matt Smethurst, "Ordinary Cook, Unlikely Hero," thegospelcoalition.org, November 3, 2013.

QUESTIONS OF THE HEART

I always like to see the Big Picture before jumping into the details. So here it is! We'll unpack what all of this means in the next chapters in this section.

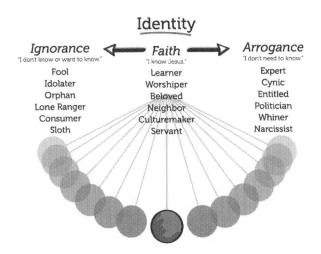

TERMINOLOGY

Who am I? They mock me, these lonely questions of mine, Whoever I am, thou knowest, O God, I am thine!
—Dietrich Bonhoeffer, *Letters and Papers from Prison*

One of the major difficulties in our culture today is the compulsion to redefine everything. So I have included definitions for the terminology used in the *Questions of the Heart*.

Identity

Everyone is talking about identity: the church, psychologists, techies, and businesses. Just read this quote from one of my favorite business books, *Brains on Fire*:

> If you are struggling with your identity, then you're probably struggling with everything else. However, once you really know who you are and why you exist, everything else becomes clear as day: How you should engage people. What tools you should use. How you should reframe the conversation. What conversations

you should even be participating in. Everything starts with identity.[1]

Am I right? Sounds like something you would pull off a theology bookshelf. "Finding your identity" is the new catchphrase and has opened up a pandora's box of definitions, so we need to build a biblical framework of definitions if we are going to speak about true identity.

Identity is how we define ourselves in relation to God, to others and the world around us. Identity is at the core of our existence, a combination of how we think about ourselves, feel about ourselves and how we act. Our identity shapes what we value, our meaning of life and our purpose. Most of us seek and find our identity in the world around us—people, places, professions and possessions. The culture we live in has a significant influence on our identity—especially where we live. Sarah Williams Goldhage taught for ten years at Harvard University's Graduate School of Design. She writes:

> Urban spaces, landscapes, and buildings—even small and modest ones— profoundly influence human lives. They shape our cognitions, emotions, and actions, and even powerfully influence our wellbeing. They actually help constitute our very sense of ourselves, our sense of identity.[2]

Whether it be the urban hipster vibe or the manicured gated community of the suburbs, we all are influenced by the values of our surroundings. In *Death by*

Suburbs, David Goetz challenges those in the suburbs to find a thicker identity:

> The outward physical world of SUVs and minivans, drearily earth-toned subdivisions, golden retrievers and chocolate labs, and endless Saturday morning soccer games is only one dimension. There's another dimension or two. This much thicker world is a world in which I am alive to God and alive to others, a world in which what I don't yet own defines me. It's a higher existence, a plane where I am not the sum total of my house size, SUV, vacations, kid's report cards—and that which I still need to acquire.[3]

Because we are created in the image of God, our identity can't be bound to this world. It can only be found beyond it. In the aptly named book *Beyond Identity,* Dick Keyes writes:

> Humans will always compute their values in terms of something, whether that something is worthy or able to bestow value on them or not. It is only when people reach beyond humankind that they can get any conclusive affirmation of themselves.[4]

For us to make sense of who we are, we must look to the one who is both Beyond and Immanuel. Daniel Darling writes:

> Our dignity flows from and is rooted in the truth that we are like God. You are more than simply the sum of

your parts. You are not merely a highly evolved mammal. You are not just a collection of atoms. You are not just what others see or the combination of others' verdicts on you. You are made in the image of God: crowned, the psalmist writes, "with glory and honor." (Psalm 8:5)[5]

Pascal summarizes:

Not only do we know God by Jesus Christ alone, but we know ourselves only by Jesus Christ. We know life and death only through Jesus Christ. Apart from Jesus Christ, we do not know what is our life, nor our death, nor God, nor ourselves.[6]

For you formed my inward parts; you knitted me together in my mother's womb. I praise you, for I am fearfully and wonderfully made. Wonderful are your works; my soul knows it very well.
Ps. 139:13–14

But you are a chosen race, a royal priesthood, a holy nation, a people for his own possession, that you may proclaim the excellencies of him who called you out of darkness into his marvelous light. Once you were not a people, but now you are God's people; once you had not received mercy, but now you have received mercy.
1 Pet. 2:9–10

But whatever gain I had, I counted as loss for the sake of Christ. Indeed, I count everything as loss because of the

*surpassing worth of knowing Christ Jesus my Lord. For
his sake I have suffered the loss of all things and count
them as rubbish, in order that I may gain Christ and be
found in him, not having a righteousness of my own that
comes from the law, but that which comes through faith
in Christ, the righteousness from God that depends on
faith*
Phil. 3:7–9

---

1. Robbin Phillips, Greg Cordell, Geno Church and Spike Jones, *Brains on Fire: Igniting Powerful, Sustainable, Word of Mouth Movements* (Hoboken: John Wiley & Sons Inc, 2010), 118–119.

2. Sarah Williams Goldhagen, *Welcome to Your World: How the Built Environment Shapes Our Lives* (New York: Harper Collins, 2017), XXIII.

3. David L. Goetz, *Death by Suburb: How to Keep the Suburbs from Killing Your Soul* (New York: HarperCollins Publishing, 2006), 12–13.

4. Dick Keyes, *Beyond Identity: Finding Yourself in the Image and Character of God* (Switzerland: Destinée Media, 2012), 13.

5. Daniel Darling, *The Dignity Revolution: Reclaiming God's Rich Vision for Humanity* (Charlotte: The Good Book Company, 2018), 23.

6. Blaise, Pascal, *Pensées* (Thoughts) translated by W. F. Trotter in The Harvard Classics, Volume 48 (New York: P. F. Collier & Sons, 1995), 177.

POSTURES TOWARD GOD

Identity

Ignorance ⬅━━━ *Faith* ━━━➡ *Arrogance*
"I don't know or want to know."   "I know Jesus."   "I don't need to know."

"Quit slouching! Do you want to be stuck that way forever?!"

My mother constantly used these threats to urge me toward good posture. Even now, I can hear her voice as I pull my shoulders back to sit up straight. The consequences then were minimal—a reprimand or a tight squeeze of the arm.

The consequences are much weightier when it comes to a bad spiritual posture towards God. In this chapter, we are going to look at three central postures that people take in dealing with God: faith, ignorance, and arrogance. You don't want to be stuck with a bad posture toward God. The consequences are eternal.

Faith

Charles Spurgeon writes, "Faith is believing that Christ is what he is said to be, and that he will do what he has promised to do, and then to expect this of him."[1] The strength of faith is not in how much one possesses, but in the greatness of the object it is in. Therefore, believers can have the faith of a mustard seed, as long as they are trusting in Christ. Faith trusts his Word to define all of reality and to find one's identity in him. Faith trusts that his Word is truth and seeks to live according to it in humble reliance. Biblical faith in Christ believes that he is fully God and fully man, the only begotten Son of God, the Savior of sinners, the Author and Perfecter of our faith—the Alpha and Omega.

We have seen that Scripture declares that every question of the heart is answered in him. Faith cries out, My life is hidden in Christ, and I count everything as loss for the surpassing worth of knowing Christ Jesus my Lord.

In his commentary on Romans, Martin Luther writes:

> Faith... is a divine work in us. It changes us and makes us to be born anew of God (John 1); it kills the old Adam and makes altogether different men, in heart and spirit, mind and powers, and it brings with it the Holy Ghost. Faith is a living, unshakeable confidence in God's grace; it is so certain that someone would die a thousand times for it. This kind of trust in and

knowledge of God's grace makes a person joyful, confident, and happy with regard to God and all creatures. This is what the Holy Spirit does by faith. Through faith, a person will do good to everyone without coercion, willingly and happily; he will serve everyone, suffer everything for the love and praise of God, who has shown him such grace. It is as impossible to separate works from faith as burning and shining from fire.[2]

Faith is always attached to repentance. They are the two-step dance of the Gospel. John Murray explains, "The faith that is unto salvation is a penitent faith and the repentance that is unto life is a believing repentance … saving faith is permeated with repentance and repentance is permeated with saving faith."[3] By faith, we turn away from our false identities and turn to Christ. When our eyes are opened in faith to see Jesus rightly, we can't help but cast aside the empty idols that we once upheld. Jesus becomes precious to those who believe, who put their faith in him alone for salvation and life.

For I am not ashamed of the gospel, for it is the power of God for salvation to everyone who believes, to the Jew first and also to the Greek. For in it the righteousness of God is revealed from faith for faith, as it is written, "The righteous shall live by faith."
Ro. 1:16–17

I have been crucified with Christ. It is no longer I who live, but Christ who lives in me. And the life I now live in

the flesh I live by faith in the Son of God, who loved me
and gave himself for me.
Ga. 2:20

Ignorance

While America's evangelical Christians are rightly concerned about the secular worldview's rejection of biblical Christianity, we ought to give some urgent attention to a problem much closer to home—biblical illiteracy in the church.

Researchers George Gallup and Jim Castelli put the problem squarely: Americans revere the Bible—but, by and large, they don't read it. And because they don't read it, they have become a nation of biblical illiterates.

How bad is it?

Researchers tell us that it's worse than most could imagine.

Fewer than half of all adults can name the four gospels. Many Christians cannot identify more than two or three of the disciples. According to data from the Barna Research Group, 60 percent of Americans can't name even five of the Ten Commandments. "No wonder people break the Ten Commandments all the time. They don't know what they are," said George Barna, president of the firm. The bottom line? "Increasingly, America is biblically illiterate."[4]

Not knowing the truth of the Scriptures means that we will approach life in ignorance.

Ignorance has a few different postures toward God and others. One posture is that we just flat-out ignore them. Ambivalence and foolishness mark this attitude toward life—we have no desire to change. Things are fine the way they are, and I don't want to think about or put any effort into considering otherwise. We couldn't care less about meaning or the future, and we live for the moment allowing whatever comes our way to define us. Don't buck my status quo!

The other posture of ignorance is where we genuinely don't understand or we have only been privy to one way of life. It's not that we are passive in the pursuit of our identity. We've just been looking in the wrong places, not allowing anyone to guide us. In Luke's gospel, Zechariah said that Jesus came to give light to those who sit in darkness and in the shadow of death, to guide their feet into the way of peace. Sometimes ignorance is due to being sinned against, leaving us in such deep gloom without hope that we can't find our way out and think that God doesn't care at all. Ignorance takes on many faces, but in the end it is pride.

The fear of the LORD is the beginning of knowledge;
fools despise wisdom and instruction.
Prov. 1:7

Poverty and disgrace come to him who ignores instruc-
tion, but whoever heeds reproof is honored.
Prov. 13:18

Arrogance

Arrogance is the posture where we think more highly of ourselves than we ought. We promote ourselves over others, even above God. I know all that I need to know. I am fine without God. I am the captain of my destiny and don't need the God crutch. My way is the right way, and if you don't like it then tough.

Arrogance is a superiority complex expressed in every realm: spiritual, moral, familial, political, social, racial, or intellectual. We believe we are the main character in the story. Donald Miller was once challenged about his arrogance, and he wrote:

> He said to me I was a tree in a story about a forest, and that it was arrogant of me to believe any differently. And he told me the story of the forest is better than the story of the tree.[5]

To the arrogant person, everything revolves around what they want and relationships are just a means to that end. Arrogance breeds anger, abuse, slander, and greed. Arrogance is big-headed pride.

In *Mere Christianity*, C. S. Lewis points out that arrogant pride is always competitive. He writes:

> Pride is essentially competitive—pride gets no pleasure out of having something, only out of having more of it than the next man. We say that people are proud of being rich, or clever, or good-looking, but they are not. They are proud of being richer, or cleverer, or better-

looking than others. If everyone else became equally rich, or clever, or good-looking there would be nothing to be proud about. It is the comparison that makes you proud: the pleasure of being above the rest.[6]

The pride of arrogance always has to one-up the person next to them. As the Pharisee prayed in Luke 18:9–12, *"God, I thank you that I am not like other men, extortioners, unjust, adulterers, or even like this tax collector."*

Everyone who is arrogant in heart is an abomination to the LORD; be assured, he will not go unpunished.
Prov. 16:5

I will punish the world for its evil, and the wicked for their iniquity; I will put an end to the pomp of the arrogant, and lay low the pompous pride of the ruthless.
Is. 13:11

---

1. Charles Hadden Spurgeon, *All of Grace* (Chicago: Moody Press, n. d.), 47.
2. Martin Luther, *Commentary on Romans* (Grand Rapids: Zondervan Publishing, 1954), 108.
3. John Murray, *Redemption—Accomplished and Applied* (Grand Rapids: Wm. B. Eerdmans Publishing Co., 1955), 113.
4. Albert Mohler, "The Scandal of Biblical Illiteracy: It's Our Problem," January 20, 2016, https:// albertmohler.-com/2016/01/20/the-scandal-of-biblical-illiteracy-its-our-problem-4/.
5. Donald Miller, *A Million Miles in a Thousand Years: What I Learned Editing My Life* (Nashville: Thomas Nelson, 2009), 198.
6. C. S. Lewis, *Mere Christianity* (New York: Touchstone, 1996), 109–112.

OUR IDENTITY BY FAITH

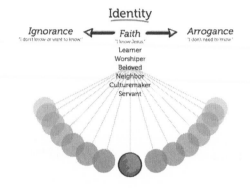

Identity

Ignorance ← *Faith* → *Arrogance*
"I don't know or want to know." "I know Jesus." "I don't need to know."

Learner
Worshiper
Beloved
Neighbor
Culturemaker
Servant

It is a nuisance when our car gets knocked out of alignment from a pothole, and even worse when it happens to our spine because of an accident. We don't hesitate to take our vehicle to a mechanic or to make an appointment with a doctor to get realigned.

How in the world then can we go a whole lifetime with our identity out of alignment? The answer is sin. We would rather wobble from side to side in ignorance or be hunched over in defiance than to go to God to be straighten out. The biblical term for being righted by God is "justification."

God does this as an act of grace through the righteousness of Jesus Christ, which he imputes to us. Jesus forgives us of our unrighteousness and credits us with his righteousness. Our identity can only be aligned to God by grace through faith in Christ's righteousness alone.

Once we find our true identity, we continue to grow in his righteousness. The Bible calls this ongoing realignment work "sanctification." In this chapter, we are going to discover what our true identity looks like as Jesus transforms us into learners, worshipers, beloved, neighbors, culturemakers, and servants.

Learner

We are all learners—always learning something from someone and the world around us. Jesus' term for the learner is a "disciple." The key is to stay a learner, avoiding  ignorance or becoming a self-proclaimed expert. Austin Kleon states:

> Amateurs might lack formal training, but they're all lifetime learners, and they make a point of learning in the open, so that others can learn from their failures and successes. Sometimes, amateurs have more to

teach us than experts. The world is changing at such a
rapid rate that it's turning us all into amateurs. Even
for professionals, the best way to flourish is to retain
an amateur's spirit and embrace uncertainty and the
unknown.[1]

We typically accumulate knowledge from whatever
comes our way without sorting through it with discernment. The tough work is figuring out if it is true or not.
All truth is God's truth, but there is much falsehood
masquerading around as light. God has revealed himself
through general revelation in creation, the special revelation of God's Word, and the embodied revelation
through Jesus Christ. In a culture of many stories, we
find great comfort and hope in the truth of God's meta-
narrative revealed in the Old and New Testaments. This
means that we must ultimately bring our questions to
the Bible to find out what God has to say about all
things for this life and the life to come.

Without the Holy Spirit, we could never believe in
Christ nor understand the Scriptures. By the Spirit's
illumination of the Word, we behold the Truth. As
learners, we read, listen to, meditate on, memorize, and
study the Word of God by faith. We take the posture of a
learner at the feet of Jesus, rather than a colleague
sitting side-by-side choosing what we want to believe or
as a critic, making judgements on the validity of God's
Word. Mary sat at the feet of Jesus, and he commended
her for choosing the one needful thing—to be a learner.
He would not take it away from her, nor will he take it
away from us.

Come to me, all who labor and are heavy laden, and I will give you rest. Take my yoke upon you, and learn from me, for I am gentle and lowly in heart, and you will find rest for your souls.
Matt. 11:28–29

All Scripture is breathed out by God and profitable for teaching, for reproof, for correction, and for training in righteousness, that the man/woman of God may be competent, equipped for every good work.
2 Tim. 3:16–17

To know wisdom and instruction, to understand words of insight, to receive instruction in wise dealing, in right-eousness, justice, and equity; to give prudence to the simple, knowledge and discretion to the youth— Let the wise hear and increase in learning, and the one who understands obtain guidance, to understand a proverb and a saying, the words of the wise and their riddles. The fear of the LORD is the beginning of knowledge; fools despise wisdom and instruction.
Prov. 1:1–7

———

One afternoon at a church planting conference, a bunch of us went bowling to blow off some steam. Dony St. Germaine brought a few of his new Haitian recruits to join us. As most of us were cutting up together, these men were pulling out their small Bibles to memorize a passage or two in between their turns to bowl. Their intensity to learn truth and their love for the Scriptures inspired us all.

In an article on biblical meditation, Tim Keller recounts Jonathan Edwards' joy in spending time in the Scriptures:

In reading [the Scripture] I seemed often to see so much light, that I could not get along in reading— almost every sentence seemed to be full of wonders.... I... found, from time to time, an inward sweetness, that used, as it were, to carry me away in my contemplations. I felt alone... sweetly conversing with Christ and wrapped and swallowed up in God.[2]

Worshiper

Author James K. A. Smith writes, "We can't not worship because we can't not love something as ultimate. To be human is to be a liturgical animal, a creature whose loves are shaped by our worship. And worship isn't optional."[3] We are created for worship and our identity is a formation of our worship, so sharing our faith is more about worship than missions. John Piper aptly states:

Missions is not the ultimate goal of the church. Worship is. Missions exists because worship doesn't. Worship is ultimate, not missions, because God is ultimate, not man. When this age is over, and the countless millions of the redeemed fall on their faces before the throne of God, missions will be no more. It is a temporary necessity. But worship abides forever. So worship is the fuel and goal of missions.[4]

Matt Redmon writes, "Worship is always in reply to revelation. As we begin to see the all-deserving worth of God, it produces an all-consuming response in us— every thought, word and deed submitted in reply to His Lordship. It is a worship with a price, a living sacrifice."[5] Worship is a way of life, where we behold our God and offer ourselves as a living sacrifice. Living by faith day to day is our spiritual act of worship that culminates together with God's people on the Lord's Day. As worshipers, we praise and adore him for his faithfulness, give thanks for what he had done and is doing, seek to obey his Word, and ask him for grace to walk in a manner worthy of his Name. Worship is the very rhythm of our lives.

Jesus meets a Samaritan Woman at a well and they have a conversation about worship. He tells her that the Father is seeking those who will worship him in spirit and truth. Bob Kauflin expounds on this conversation:

> The fact that Jesus had this conversation with an immoral woman in an obscure village should tell us something. God isn't seeking worshipers only among the significant and popular people, the successful and powerful ones. The Maker of the universe is seeking true worshipers among us all.

But why is God seeking something? Surely the all-knowing, all-seeing One doesn't lose things. And it's not as though a self-sufficient God has any needs. Why would God seek anything?

We seek what's important to us. We seek what has value. And God is seeking true worshipers—because true worshipers matter to God.[6]

We were created to worship God, but we are fallen creatures now. We have chosen to worship created things rather than the Creator. Our heart is a "perpetual forge [factory] of idols."[7] In sin, we will worship anything and everything. The prophet Isaiah tells us that the nature of worship has the effect where we actually become like what we worship, either our idols or more like our God.

In true worship, our ignorance, arrogance, deception, idolatry, brokenness and the burden of sin are lifted. We are freed to be who God created us to be and to experience the weight of his glory—his holiness, his power, his love and his grace. It is both invigorating and humbling. Through worship God changes us more and more into his likeness, and we willingly offer our lives as a living sacrifice to his honor and praise. A true worshiper fills her mind with the Scriptures, the lyrics of the Gospel, and the Spirit makes the melody of the Gospel sing deeply in her heart.

Ascribe to the Lord the glory due his name; worship the Lord in the splendor of holiness.
Ps. 29:2

*Oh come, let us worship and bow down; let us kneel
before the LORD, our Maker! For he is our God, and we
are the people of his pasture, and the sheep of his hand.*
Ps. 95:6–7

*I appeal to you therefore, brothers, by the mercies of God,
to present your bodies as a living sacrifice, holy and
acceptable to God, which is your spiritual worship.*
Ro. 12:1

———

When I worked in a Korean Church in St. Louis, there was a high school kid I met right away. Everyone said, "He's a rough one. I don't know if you'll be able to reach him."

I love a challenge and said, "Game On. Get him, Lord!"

I started leaning into his life and listening—playing golf, getting breakfast together and just hanging out. He was a skeptic, but God had other plans.

One morning, we were at Einstein's Bagels talking, and he said, "Kevin, the Bible is just an archaic old book and isn't relevant today. My problem is that I don't do what I'm supposed to do, and I keep doing the things that I shouldn't do."

I told him to turn to Romans 7:15–25 and read it. As he was reading, he was struck with fear and trembling. The one true living God had spoken to him. At a weekend retreat a few weeks later, I found him sitting in a dark room alone. I plopped down in a chair next to him, and he poured out his heart and his sin. I told him he needed to tell God all this in prayer.

He replied, "I don't know how to pray like that."

I said, "Just talk to him from your heart."

After a long silence and then sobbing, He began to pray, and the heavens opened up. After hearing his honest and raw prayer of faith and repentance, I asked God to teach me how to worship and pray like that. He had been dragged to church by his mom most of his life but that night, he saw who he was and beheld who God was. He worshiped in spirit and truth. His life was never the same and neither was mine. He set his satisfaction in Christ and is one of the most generous kingdom-minded men I know.

———

When I was planting a church in Raleigh, North Carolina, I had built a friendship with a homeless heroin addict who had AIDS. I spent so much time trying to help him, but over and over he would manipulate me and lie to me. After years of sitting in rehabs and detox centers with him, I realized I needed to quit trying to save him in my own strength. That night is as clear as it was twenty years ago. I stood toe to toe with him ready to throw down because I was so angry and tired. I gave him a hug outside the emergency room and with deep agony I said goodbye. I was filled with so many emotions as I sat weeping in my car. When I turned the car on, Rich Mullins came blaring through the speakers singing over and over:

> My Deliverer is coming,
> My Deliverer is standing by.
> My Deliverer is coming,
> My Deliverer is standing by.[8]

I began hopeless, and I ended up shouting at the top of my lungs in praise for Jesus. He is always standing by, and no crisis is too big for his deliverance. He is coming! I worshiped in spirit and truth that night. Sometimes we have to be brought to the end of ourselves for true worship to erupt.

Beloved

God calls us his beloved, his family, his treasured possession, the apple of his eye, his children, and many other unexpected and unde-  served familial endearments. Embracing this truth about God's gracious love is where life flourishes. Brennan Manning wrote:

> Living in awareness of our belovedness is the axis around which the Christian life revolves. Being the

beloved is our identity, the core of our existence. It is not merely a lofty thought, an inspiring idea, or one name among many. It is the name by which God knows us and the way He relates to us.[9]

We must grasp the truth that God truly loves us not because we are beautiful, smart, artistic, athletic, or useful but simply because of his great love and pleasure. We must also understand the tremendous cost of his love.

While we were enemies, God chose us and demonstrated the greatest act of love for us by sending his Son to die in our stead. It is through this foundation that we can build an understanding of who we are and the calling that God has for our lives.

J. I. Packer explains:

If you want to judge how well a person understands Christianity, find out how much he makes of the thought of being God's child, and having God as his Father. If this is not the thought that prompts and controls his worship and prayers and his whole outlook on life, it means that he does not understand Christianity very well at all.[10]

This takes faith to believe that God loves us more than we could ever imagine. Singer songwriter Jess Ray summarizes our struggle to grasp God's love: "It may be too good to be understood, but it's not too good to be true."[11]

The Gospel is not only the good news that we are

forgiven but that we are now dearly loved as a child of God. One of the greatest needs of a heart is to love and to be loved. Jesus taught his disciples one of the most significant aspects of the Christian life when they asked him how to pray. He didn't teach his disciples to pray to "his Father" but to "Our Father who art in heaven," uniting us as brothers and sisters, fellow children of God.

We are told in the epistle to the Romans that we can now cry out "Abba Father." This is not so much a term of endearment as a child's only resort when helpless and beyond an ability to cope.

My mentor, Adrian, told me one of his childhood stories. His older brothers would go out and play ball near the house, and some bullies drove up and began harassing them. Adrian wasn't big enough the help, so he did the only thing he could. He yelled at the top of his lungs, "Daaaddd!!!" And his daddy came a running, and so did the bullies.

We have that kind of access and relationship in the midst of any crisis. We have a Heavenly Father that we can cry out at any time, "Abba, Father." We can enter his throne room of grace as dearly loved sons and daughters in our time of need.

I have loved you with an everlasting love; I have drawn you with loving-kindness. I will build you up again and you will be rebuilt, O Virgin Israel. Again you will take up your tambourines and go out to dance with the joyful.
Jer. 31:3–4

I will not leave you as orphans; I will come to you.
John 14:18

How great is the love the Father has lavished on us, that we should be called children of God! And that is what we are!
1 John 3:1

––––––

When I was teaching our first new members class, the room was predominantly filled with college-educated adults with a smattering of others. There was one gentleman in his sixties who had been imprisoned for most of his adulthood, severely abused and had the mind of a twelve-year-old. He would wander the streets most days but on Sunday he was at our church in his purple sweatpants, cowboy boots, and sports coat. I was teaching on the doctrine of election, which was something he had never heard before.

He stopped the whole class and said, "So in your opinion God has loved me before I was born."

I said, "It's not my opinion but what the Word of God says. Everyone open your Bibles to Ephesians 1." I asked him to read.

He began to read in a child-like manner:

Blessed be the God and Father of our Lord Jesus Christ, who has blessed us in Christ with every spiritual blessing in the heavenly places, even as he chose us in him before the foundation of the world, that we should be holy and blameless before him. In love he predestined us for adoption to himself as sons through Jesus Christ, according to the purpose of his will, to the praise of his glorious grace, with which he has blessed us in the Beloved. Eph. 1:3–7

As he read, *"he chose us in him before the foundation of the world.... In love he predestined us for adoption to himself as sons,"* he wept, and wept, and wept, and couldn't speak until finally He broke the silence, "I can't believe this. Is it really true? Wow! He loves me as a son? Wow! Wow!"

There wasn't a dry eye in the room. Everyone became child-like again in awe of God's love.

———

Some friends of ours decided to adopt one of the 153 million children in orphanages around the world.[12] As a young married couple, they wanted to show a little one the same kind of love that God had shown them in Christ. Their search landed them with a boy in Azerbaijan, but there were potential risks. The pictures revealed an abnormally shaped head, which could mean all kinds of health issues. Most doctors advised them not to proceed. One doctor dissented. He had been a doctor on the mission field where he dealt with third-world orphanages. He told them that many times the children's heads are misshaped because they are not held and are left lying in their cribs for days on end.

This report only deepened this couples' love, and they continued with the adoption. They reasoned that God had loved them despite their misshaping. Their boy is now in college, and his brother, who they adopted from Korea, is finishing up high school.

Neighbor

When I was tucking my son in bed one night, I asked him, "Where is your favorite place?" Expecting to hear the zoo, the beach or something like that, I was undone when he answered. "No Daddy. My favorite place is right here next to you."

We were designed for family and community—to take great delight in being next to each other. In a culture where the concept of family is so distorted, it is crucial for believers to be great neighbors. Jay Pathak and Dave Runyon start their book, *The Art of Neighboring*, by asking:

> What if the solution to our society's biggest issues has been right under our noses for the past two thousand years? When Jesus was asked to reduce everything in the Bible into one command he said: Love God with everything you have and love your neighbor as

yourself. What if he meant that we should love our actual neighbors? You know, the people who live right next door. Could it be that simple? [13]

Loving our neighbors flows out of our apprehension of God's lavish love for us.

Loving people means taking the time to unpack the truth of the Gospel in the midst of the mundane, the challenges, the joys, and the sorrows of everyday life. Jesus said the weighty matters of loving God and loving our neighbors are justice, mercy, and faithfulness. All the law and the prophets hang on these things. Being good neighbors is living out these weightier matters in our community—to love mercy, to do justly, and to walk humbly with our God.

Justice is giving each person his or her due as one created in the image of God. Mercy loves the forgotten and rejected of society. It also entails even loving those who have sinned against us. Faithfulness is doing it consistently for the long haul to the glory of God.

Neighboring is practicing the presence of those around us. Mercy enters into the life of others with grace, provision and love. Hospitality invites people into our lives to share in all the good things God has entrusted to us. It takes faith to let God choose our friendships. In loving our neighbors, we show the world who Christ is. Like the Good Samaritan, we are to stop and take the time to invest in our neighbors. Scott Sauls asks the questions in *Irresistible Faith*, "What would it look like for us to become those who live most beautifully, love most deeply, and serve most faithfully in the places where we live, work and play?... What would it look like for Christians to become an irresistible force again, even among their non-believing friends, colleagues, and neighbors?"[14] In *Search to Belong*, Francis Schaeffer writes, "Our relationship with each other is the criterion the world uses to judge whether our message is truthful—Christian community is the final apologetic."[15]

> *If you really fulfill the royal law according to the Scripture, "You shall love your neighbor as yourself," you are doing well.*
> Ja. 2:8

> *Put on then, as God's chosen ones, holy and beloved, compassionate hearts, kindness, humility, meekness, and patience, bearing with one another and, if one has a complaint against another, forgiving each other; as the Lord has forgiven you, so you also must forgive. And above all these put on love, which binds everything together in perfect harmony.*
> Col. 3:12–14

Layla, one of my friend's daughters, noticed a girl at school who sat by herself every day at lunch, so she went over to join her. The girl was deaf which made communicating difficult. Layla began teaching herself sign language, so she could love her new friend.

Layla began taking her new friend to her church youth group and signing the messages for her to understand. The Lord used this thoughtful young girl's desire to be a good neighbor, and he called her friend to be his very own. Just as God came down and met us in our struggle, Layla sat down and became the friend who changed this girl's life forever

---

Whenever we moved into a new neighborhood, we would throw a "Come Meet Your New Neighbor" party. We were always surprised that almost everyone we invited would come. Each set of neighbors was different though. In one of the neighborhoods, we were shocked that most of them had lived there for over a decade and never knew each other. Breaking the ice this way started many friendships with single moms, Muslims, elderly couples, various races, and children. It also opened up many conversations around the questions of the heart.

Culturemaker

In his seminal work, *The Rise of the Creative Class*, Richard Florida points out that creativity is the new commodity of this generation. The Scripture takes it a

bit further by declaring that
creativity, the art of culture
making, is not only a central
commodity for this generation
but has been and always will
be for every generation. Andy
Crouch challenges Christians
to champion culture making

rather than simply condemning, critiquing, copying, or
consuming culture. He offers a more biblical alternative
posture:

> We are to be creators and cultivators. Or to put it more
> poetically, we are artists and gardeners after the
> contemplation, the artist and the gardener both adopt
> a posture of purposeful work. They bring their
> creativity and effort to their calling. They are acting in
> the image of One who spoke a world into being and
> stooped down to form creatures from the dust. They
> are creaturely creators, tending and shaping the world
> that original Creator made. I wonder what we
> Christians are known for in the world outside our
> churches. Are we known as critics, consumers, copiers,
> condemners of culture? I'm afraid so. Why aren't we
> known as cultivators—people who tend and nourish
> what is best in human culture, who do the hard and
> painstaking work to preserve the best of what people
> before us have done? Why aren't we known as creators
> —people who dare to think and do something that has
> never been thought or done before, something that

makes the world more welcoming and thrilling and beautiful?[16]

God has called us to be culturemakers and not just consumers of culture. We are to create culture that reflects the kingdom of God. Our prayer must be, "On earth as it is in heaven." By using our gifts, skills, resources, and time, we can bring the Kingdom to bear in our neighborhoods, workplace, and community. God has given us the great privilege of discovery and creativity to pursue the city beautiful. We should shape the culture of business, education, the arts, medicine, politics, agriculture, science, and athletics for the glory of God. Our bottom line is not profit but the glory of God throughout all of creation. Our work and play is sacred space just like it is in the church. Instead of whining about our culture or consuming whatever the world sets before us, we are to transform our culture by faith.

At a church planting workshop, one of the leaders challenged us to think. He asked, "If the kingdom of God were to come in its fullness, what would change the most about your community?" Shouldn't this be the question that every Christian and church is asking? Then we must come together and ask God to use us to do it.

And let the beauty of the Lord our God be upon us;
confirm and establish the work of our hands—yes, the
work of our hands, confirm and establish it.
Ps. 90:17

I have filled him with the Spirit of God, with ability and intelligence, with knowledge and all craftsmanship, to devise artistic designs, to work in gold, silver, and bronze, in cutting stones for setting, and in carving wood, to work in every craft.
Ex. 31:3–5

For we are his workmanship, created in Christ Jesus for good works, which God prepared beforehand, that we should walk in them.
Eph. 2:10

———

Wayne is one of my friends, and he is an elder in the church. He is an architect and an artist. He is brilliant at taking dreams and making them a reality. The thoughtfulness and care he takes with those who entrust him to design their home is a real testimony of his calling. As an architect, he primarily designs spectacular homes, dwellings for life, rest, memories, and love. As an artist, he paints with a palette knife thoughtfully layering colors, texture, and beauty. In his words:

I enjoy painting because it is personal. There is not a client. As an architect, I have the privilege of connecting/working with people to make buildings and spaces and places. In painting, I find solitude and the chance to think, reflect, and express.

If you ask him about a house he designed or a painting that he is displaying, his eyes light up and a smile emerges on his face. He will tell the tale of the journey and the story behind the masterpiece. Wayne is a culturemaker transforming the lives of those he calls friends, the built environment in which he resides, and the canvas he paints on.

Like many little girls, my two daughters wanted to be ballerinas as soon as they could walk and twirl. When we moved to Lexington, we looked for a dance company. We were thrilled to find the South Carolina Christian Dance Theater. The leaders of this dance company wed quality dance with a Christian Worldview. They created breath-taking performances that share the Gospel message, and they teach the girls to glorify God through movement. My oldest daughter traveled with them to Argentina and Africa sharing her faith in word and dance. They are beautiful culturemakers.

Servant

I've always appreciated Michael Card's music and his books. Perhaps you think it's dated, and it might be. His writing is lesser known, but always on point. He has a knack for getting to the heart of Jesus, and this quote is

a great example of how he pictures
Jesus' servanthood. He writes:

> Jesus said, "The Son of Man came to serve not to be
> served." The King of Kings took on flesh and dwelt
> among us, endured the shame of the cross and bore
> the penalty of our sin unto death—the greatest act of
> service known to mankind. When we take the posture
> of a servant, we are most like Jesus. The disciples, like
> most artists and musicians, argue, "Who is the
> greatest?" And Jesus rises, still hungry, from his own
> supper and demonstrates what true greatness is. In the
> upside-down kingdom, true greatness is found in the
> servant's kneeling with the basin and the towel.[17]

Serving our friends and our community means that
we kneel down and enter into its brokenness, we correct
that which is wrong, and we care for the least of them.
In a competitive world chasing after numero uno, we
choose the lowly place and give our lives away so that
others may see Jesus. The first will be last, and the last
will be first. In *Faithmapping*, Daniel Montgomery and
Mike Cosper show how God uses the underdogs to
reveal his greatness. They write:

> Through a handful of relatively unimportant people
> who suffered, served, and died, God changed the
> world, making himself available to you and me and

setting a trajectory to make all things new. When Jesus takes hold of our hearts, he plants that same underdog spirit in us, inviting us into a life where we discover that everything about how the world sees greatness is backwards, that it's truly better to serve than be served, to give than receive, to be lowly rather than great. This underdog spirit is a new identity: the gospel makes us servants, and our service is all about the gospel.[18]

And Jesus called them to him and said to them, "You know that those who are considered rulers of the Gentiles lord it over them, and their great ones exercise authority over them. But it shall not be so among you. But whoever would be great among you must be your servant, and whoever would be first among you must be slave of all.
Mark 10:42–44

For you were called to freedom, brothers. Only do not use your freedom as an opportunity for the flesh, but through love serve one another.
Ga. 5:13

Is not this the kind of fasting I have chosen: to loose the chains of injustice and untie the cords of the yoke, to set the oppressed free and break every yoke? Is it not to share your food with the hungry and to provide the poor wanderer with shelter— when you see the naked, to clothe him, and not to turn away from your own flesh and blood? Then your light will break forth like the dawn, and your healing will quickly appear; then your

righteousness will go before you, and the glory of the LORD will be your rear guard. Then you will call, and the LORD will answer; you will cry for help, and he will say: "Here am I. If you do away with the yoke of oppression, with the pointing finger and malicious talk, and if you spend yourselves in behalf of the hungry and satisfy the needs of the oppressed, then your light will rise in the darkness, and your night will become like the noonday. The LORD will guide you always; he will satisfy your needs in a sun-scorched land and will strengthen your frame. You will be like a well-watered garden, like a spring whose waters never fail. Your people will rebuild the ancient ruins and will raise up the age-old foundations; you will be called Repairer of Broken Walls, Restorer of Streets with Dwellings."
Is. 58:6–12

———

Elvis is a young professional in the IT industry. Elvis is his nickname since no one can pronounce his given Indian name. He has kept it, because it makes people smile. One of my friends met Elvis on an airplane. Their conversation turned to spiritual things and then to the gospel. The Lord used that conversation, and my friend asked him to read Tim Keller's book *Prodigal God*. He also invited him to visit our church. He came over for dinner and told us how the book was challenging his thinking. He grew up in a secular Hindu home. After reading Keller's book, he identified with both the younger and the elder son. Elvis came to know the Lord.

He put it this way: "I exchanged my old CPU for a new one."

He wrestled with what God would have him to do as follower of Christ. He began reading Scripture and praying for his answer. God reminded him of a hotel owner's kindness in giving him a room to live in while in college. Little by little as the economy began to crash, God put homelessness on Elvis's heart, so he chose to live in his car for a season to experience it for himself.

This led him to buy a house to share with people. Elvis slept on the couch and opened the other three rooms for those in need. As things progressed, he began to address the real problem of affordable housing for the underemployed. He went on to secure more homes for men and women with addiction. He bought an old church and turned it into a twenty-five-bed dorm for men, and he secured an apartment complex for women with children. He continues to wrestle with serving those in need and learns from each endeavor. One thing he knows is that people need to be treated as humans and have a place of peace to answer the questions of their hearts. He calls his community investment The House of Peace.

———

One of my neighbors called me one afternoon and asked if I would stop by her neighbor's house. He was an elderly gentleman who had just lost his son. I went over and offered my condolences and began a friendship with him. It wasn't but a few weeks later that his wife was diagnosed with cancer. It was the aggressive

type, and she soon passed. We walked together through those tough weeks, and I was honored to be a part of the funeral. He ended up joining our church and is a huge blessing to everyone who knows him. It all began with the servant heart of his neighbor.

---

1. Austin Kleon, *Show Your Work: 10 Ways to Share Your Creativity and Get Discovered* (New York: Workman Publishing, 2014), 16–18.
2. Tim Keller, "A Prayer Life That Nourishes Your Relationship With God," in Redeemer Report, 2010, https://www.redeemer.com/redeemer-report/article/a_prayer_life_that_nourishes_your_relationship_to_god.
3. James K. A. Smith, *You Are What You Love: The Spiritual Power of Habit* (Ada: Brazos Press, 2016), 23.
4. John Piper, *Let The Nations Be Glad: The Supremacy of God in Missions* (Ada: Baker, 2010), 15.
5. Matt Redman, *Facedown* (Bloomington: Bethany House Publishers, 2004), 57.
6. Bob Kauflin, *True Worshipers: Seeking What Matters to God* (Illinois: Crossway, 2015), 26.
7. John Calvin, *Institutes of the Christian Religion in Two Volumes* (Pennsylvania: The Westminster Press, 1970), 1.11.8.
8. "My Deliverer Lyrics." Lyrics.com. STANDS4 LLC, 2019. Web. 3 Jan. 2020, https:// www.lyrics.com/lyric/4355440/Rich+Mullins.
9. Brennan Manning, *Abba's Child: The Cry of the Heart for Intimate Belonging* (Colorado: NavPress, 2015), 84.
10. J. I. Packer, *Knowing God* (London: Hodder and Stoghton, 1973), 182.
11. *Too Good*, 2015, [CD]. Track 1 on Jess Ray, Sentimental Creatures, Self-Published.

12. SOS Children's Villages. Children's statistics, sos-usa.org.

13. Jay Pathak and Dave Runyon, *The Art of Neighboring: Building Genuine Relationship Right Outside Your Door* (Grand Rapids: Baker Books, 2012), 15–20.

14. Scott Sauls, *Irresistible Faith: Becoming the Kind of Christians the World Can't Resist* (Nashville: Thomas & Nelson, 2019), XXII.

15. Joseph Myers, *The Search to Belong: Rethinking Intimacy, Community, and Small Groups* (Michigan: Zondervan, 2003), 65.

16. Andy Crouch, *Culture Making: Recovering Our Creative Calling* (Downers Grove: InterVarsity Press, 2008), 97–98.

17. Michael Card, *Scribbling in the Sand: Christ and Creativity*

18. Daniel Montgomery and Mike Cosper, *Faithmapping: A Gospel Atlas for Your Spiritual Journey* (Wheaton: Crossway, 2013), 144.

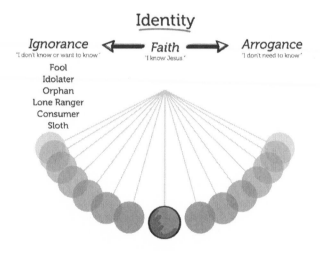

Ignorance is bliss. Or is it?

Ignorance comes in handy when you don't want to be the go-to-guy to fix someone's computer software issue or to install your next door neighbor's toilet.

Ignorance is anything but bliss when we turn a blind eye to our neighbor and God. Our identity conforms to a lie rather than being informed by the truth. When we shrug off God and his Word, we become fools, idolaters, orphans, loners, consumers, and sloths. In this chapter, we will look at how the pride of ignorance distorts our identity.

Fool

In ignorance, a simpleton doesn't know about the truth nor how to seek it out. He has an infantile mind. A fool, on the other hand, may know truth but despises instruction and discipline, living according to what is right in his own eyes. A fool doesn't want to learn and therefore is unteachable. They have settled for one perspective and have closed their minds to counsel and to the pursuit of wisdom. Anne Lamont colorfully explains:

> If we stay where we are, where we're stuck, where we're comfortable and safe, we die there. We become like mushrooms, living in the dark, with poop up to our chins. If you want to know only what you already know, you're dying. You're saying: Leave me alone; I don't mind this little rathole. It's warm and dry. Really, it's fine. When nothing new can get in, that's death. When oxygen can't find a way in, you die. But new is scary, and new can be disappointing, and confusing— we had this all figured out, and now we don't. New is life.[1]

There is also the Fool, who is the product of other fools, who have been confined to one way of thinking. They have been kept from seeing and discouraged from understanding. They may have been born into a culture that is blind to the truth, usually in another religious system. They simply have never heard or been given the opportunity to consider gospel truth. This can be a systemic ignorance forced upon its citizens or constituents. The Scripture says that the simpleton and the fool are both a product of prideful ignorance.

For the simple are killed by their turning away, and the complacency of fools destroys them; but whoever listens to me will dwell secure and will be at ease, without dread of disaster.
Prov. 1:32–33

I love entrepreneurs and the art of starting something new or renewing something that is broken. The Lord has blessed me with some great friends who are successful in business. I like to find out what makes them tick. One day in a conversation, the issue of church came up, and my friend began telling me where he attended and that it was where his wife's family had been members most of their lives. Knowing that this church did not hold to the Bible nor taught the Gospel, I asked, "If you know that this church doesn't teach truth, then why do you still take your family there and allow your kids to be shaped by it?"

He responded, "That's a good question. I guess I just don't want to rock the boat with all my in-laws. I don't want to have to deal with all the fallout."

It amazes me that marketplace leaders, who pride themselves on making great strategic decisions every day for their businesses, settle for not rocking the boat with their family's relationship with God. Talking with other business owners about their lack of involvement in church has brought out their disconnect and spiritual foolishness.

———

A new friend of mine came to America on a job assignment from overseas. He would only be here until the job was completed. As we got to know each other, I went through the *Questions of the Heart* with him. He realized that his identity was skewed, because he grew up in a culture that did not talk about Jesus Christ. He realized that he didn't know much about the Bible and Jesus, so he asked me to teach him. Ignorance isn't necessarily a willful rejection of truth. It may just be that they have never been given the chance to learn about the truth. As he went back, he was wrestling with how following Christ would disrupt his family and the cost of putting his faith in him.

Idolater

In ignorance, an idolater will worship the created rather than the Creator. They give themselves over to whatever brings them temporary satisfaction and meaning. Richard Keyes defines idolatry as "someone's obsessional preoccupations," and he goes on to say:

> An idol is something within creation that is inflated to function as a substitute for God. All sorts of things are potential idols, depending only on our attitudes and actions toward them. Idols will inevitably involve self-centeredness, self-inflation, and self-deception.[2]

Idolaters live for their near idols (the concrete and specific things that control us like a job or a person) to satisfy their far idols (power, comfort, pleasure).

Second Kings 17:33 reminds us that our worship can be a synergism of fearing God and serving idols: *"So they feared the LORD but also served their own gods, after the manner of the nations from among whom they had been carried away."* Kelly Minter reflects on this reality in her own life:

> Perhaps so many of our struggles—lack of freedom, loss of spiritual desire, slavery to image, perfectionism, confusion, and the list is infinite—had much to do with this idea of God... getting my worship on some level but my gods were getting my service."[3]

John ends his first epistle with, *"Little children, keep yourselves from idols."*

All who fashion idols are nothing, and the things they delight in do not profit.
Is. 44:9

For although they knew God, they did not honor him as God or give thanks to him, but they became futile in their thinking, and their foolish hearts were darkened. Claiming to be wise, they became fools, and exchanged the glory of the immortal God for images resembling mortal man and birds and animals and creeping things. Therefore God gave them up in the lusts of their hearts to impurity, to the dishonoring of their bodies among themselves, because they exchanged the truth about God for a lie and worshiped and served the creature rather than the Creator, who is blessed forever! Amen.
Ro. 1:21–25

———

My friend called me. He was furious.

He said, "I'm so mad. I got a call from a high school classmate yesterday. He just got a new job, and he told me he got a $600,000 signing bonus. Why him? Why not me? I mean I make good money, but I just can't shake it. I want more. This guy isn't even a Christian. Why is God blessing him and not me like that?" (He was making six digits as well.)

This opened up a long conversation about his worship of money and success that he had been struggling with—a midlife crisis. His bigger struggle though was with purpose. If he continued to rise in his present company, he knew he would have to jeopardize his character to do so. He was stuck.

———

It doesn't take long at the ballfield to see parents making idols out of their children's success. Now don't get me wrong. We should all cheer our kids on and dote on them from time to time. It gets out of hand though when a dad tries to relive his glory days or a mom lives vicariously through her daughter's youthful beauty. The idolatry of appearing to have it all together is deadly. Ugly parenting comes out when the success of our children is propping up our own ego. On many occasions, I've seen dads holding each other back when the game gets a bit intense, which leads to some heated conversations of the heart.

Orphan

In ignorance, spiritual orphans live as if they are unlovable and without value, as if God has forgotten them. They have either given up or are constantly spinning their wheels seeking the love of others. In *This is Awkward*, Sammy Rhodes confesses, "My ability to simultaneously be afraid of people while deeply trying to please them is my superpower."[4] Spiritual orphans live in perpetual fear of losing something or messing it up. They settle for surface acceptance because they are sure if people really know who they are then rejection is sure to follow. They wallow in despair, as if no one really cares about them. They deny what Scripture says about them as children of God and settle for a lie and its condemning accusations. Remember Satan is the Father of Lies and the Accuser of the brethren.

Henri Nouwen shared his own struggle:

Although claiming my true identity as a child of God, I still live as though the God to whom I am returning demands an explanation. I still think about his love as conditional and about home as a place I am not yet fully sure of. While walking home, I keep entertaining doubts about whether I will be truly welcome when I get there. As I look at my spiritual journey, my long and fatiguing trip home, I see how full it is of guilt about the past and worries about the future. I realize my failures and know that I have lost the dignity of my sonship, but I am not yet able to fully believe that where my failings are great, "grace is always greater." Still clinging to my sense of worthlessness, I project for myself a place far below that which belongs to the son....[5]

Jack Miller brought insight into the doctrine of

sonship and offered a few mindsets of an orphan. An orphan feels alone, anxious over felt needs, lives on a success/fail basis, feels condemned by others and God, is jealous of others' success, tries to earn love, and has lots of fear and little faith. A legalistic and demanding household or church, where behavior matters more than the relationship, is fertile ground for an orphan.

> So the two of them went on until they came to Bethlehem. And when they came to Bethlehem, the whole town was stirred because of them. And the women said, "Is this Naomi?" She said to them, "Do not call me Naomi; call me Mara, for the Almighty has dealt very bitterly with me. I went away full, and the LORD has brought me back empty. Why call me Naomi, when the LORD has testified against me and the Almighty has brought calamity upon me?
> Ruth 1:19–21

> Once when Jacob was cooking stew, Esau came in from the field, and he was exhausted. And Esau said to Jacob, "Let me eat some of that red stew, for I am exhausted!" (Therefore his name was called Edom.) Jacob said, "Sell me your birthright now." Esau said, "I am about to die; of what use is a birthright to me?" Jacob said, "Swear to me now." So he swore to him and sold his birthright to Jacob. Then Jacob gave Esau bread and lentil stew, and he ate and drank and rose and went his way. Thus Esau despised his birthright.
> Gen. 25:29–34

She was a latchkey teenager who followed many on social media but lacked real friendships. Clicking away on her phone mostly discouraged her because she was seeing all the fun others were having without her. She lived in the shadow of her sister, the golden child. Her parents told her they loved her but were too busy to persuade her of that truth. She hid away behind her locked bedroom door where she turned up the music and cut herself just enough to remind her that she was still alive. If it wasn't for a few good friends listening to the questions of her heart, she wouldn't be with us today.

My friend seemed to be secure in who he was, but he had been lying to his wife about how he was doing in graduate school. His grades were really struggling, but he couldn't bring himself to tell her. She didn't find out until it was almost too late. He had even dropped some classes without her knowing. He was ashamed of his failure and couldn't face her disapproval. He finally got caught in the lie. I sat listening to the questions of his heart for many nights. The pattern he revealed began with demanding parents who would only settle for the best. He lived trying to gain their approval but never could manage to impress them enough. He began to hide any failure from them or anyone else. Once he saw his crisis of identity and his orphan mindset, he was set free to engage his wife with honesty and pursue the career he always wanted.

Loner

In a culture where individualism is king, it's not surprising we are raising up a whole generation of loners. Author Jean Twenge writes, "The sadness of being alone is often the flip side of freedom and putting ourselves first."[6]

Wanting some alone time or being an introvert are not what I'm writing about. Being a loner is more about the loss of true connectivity and a disregard for the value of relationships and community. Many a loner forsakes relationships in the pursuit of professional success. It's usually too late when he realizes he has no one to enjoy all his accomplishments with.

Divorce, pressure in corporate America, transience, and busyness all contribute to loneliness. At work, it can surface as a lack of trust in others to do something that you think you can do better yourself. Relationally, it is a lack of confidence in others' ability to genuinely care and be trusted. Loners isolate themselves from true relationships not knowing how much they need others to find fulfillment in life. A loner's most prized possession is independence. This may have been spurred on by an overprotective parent or the devastating effects of abuse. It's easier and more efficient to be alone until we realize we are all alone. Brené Brown says fear is one of the main reasons for loneliness. She writes:

> But if I had to identify one core variable that drives and magnifies our compulsion to sort ourselves into factions while at the same time cutting ourselves off from real connection with other people, my answer would be fear. Fear of vulnerability. Fear of getting hurt. Fear of the pain of disconnection. Fear of criticism and failure. Fear of conflict. Fear of not measuring up. Fear.[7]

Another aspect of a loner is the avoidance of those who are different. We isolate ourselves and never venture out into the lives of those with a different socio-economic position, race, or intellect. When he was in seminary, author Mike Yankoski decided to live on the streets for five months to experience a people unlike himself, the homeless. When he sat on the sidewalks during this time, Yankoski noticed people were unwilling to look at him. He writes:

> As toddlers stumble past holding their parent's hand, they lock you in their unashamed gazes or they peek curiously out from their strollers. They haven't learned to ignore what they see, so they can actually take in the world around as it is. While kids might pretend people who don't exist do, it's parents who pretend that unwanted people who do exist don't.[8]

Ignorance of the value of true community and the value of our God-given need for relationship are two of the greatest detriments to our identity.

Then the LORD God said, "It is not good that the man should be alone; I will make him a helper fit for him."
Gen. 2:18

For the body does not consist of one member but of many. If the foot should say, "Because I am not a hand, I do not belong to the body," that would not make it any less a part of the body. And if the ear should say, "Because I am not an eye, I do not belong to the body," that would not make it any less a part of the body. If the whole body were an eye, where would be the sense of hearing? If the whole body were an ear, where would be the sense of smell? But as it is, God arranged the members in the body, each one of them, as he chose. If all were a single member, where would the body be? As it is, there are many parts, yet one body.
1 Cor. 12:14–20

A hard working business woman lost her husband and lived paycheck to paycheck. She pulled herself up by her bootstraps. As a single mother, she lived to make ends meet. Most of her life had been fighting the next battle, so she hadn't been able to nurture meaningful friendships. If truth be told, she was deathly afraid of being hurt all over again. She longs for true connection but doesn't know how to do it.

———

I met Tony in a boarding house. He had lived like a hermit for over ten years. He rarely left the building out of a crippling sense of abandonment. He was better off alone fending for himself rather than being let down by others. He had been abandoned as a child and had wandered into the back door of a brothel in his early teens. They gave him respite to do as he pleased and to cobble together a life for himself. Our church had been building relationships in the Boarding House, and he ventured out to a picnic we hosted in the front yard. Tony was one cool dude and God knitted our hearts together. He slowly responded to the love of our church and regularly attended on Sunday morning. He became our greeter and handed out bulletins with a huge grin and "Good Morning!"

Consumer

In ignorance, consumers allow culture to feed their appetites. They find pleasure and comfort predominantly in this world. They are acted upon by culture rather than being active in culture's transformation. Marketers have mastered the art of mesmerizing consumers by convincing them their lives are woefully lacking without certain products. With immediate access from our phone and digital purchasing power, we are loose cannons of consumption.

Consumers are hoarders of stuff and experiences. Alison Stuart notes:

> After the "go-go greedy 1980s, the next decade became the "What the hell do we do with all this stuff?" '90s. The answer: Self storage is now a $24 billion industry 1-800-Got-Junk started with a $700 pickup truck. In 1999, it made $1 million. In 2011, the company earned $91.5 million... three of the highest rated cable television shows today are about storing junk (*Storage Wars*), selling junk (*Pawn Stars*), and finding junk (*American Pickers*).[9]

We can't help ourselves. We buy the next gadget and dispose of it just as quickly.

If stuff fills our garages, experiences are what captures the American heart. In a Harvard Business Review, the shifting-nature of economics is explained through the evolution of the birthday cake:

> As a vestige of the agrarian economy, mothers made birthday cakes from scratch, mixing farm commodities (flour, sugar, butter, and eggs) that together cost mere dimes. As the goods-based industrial economy advanced, moms paid a dollar or two to Betty Crocker for premixed ingredients. Later, when the service economy took hold, busy parents ordered cakes from

the bakery or grocery store, which, at $10 or $15, cost ten times as much as the packaged ingredients. Now, in the time-starved 1990s, parents neither make the birthday cake nor even throw the party. Instead, they spend $100 or more to "outsource" the entire event to Chuck E. Cheese's, the Discovery Zone, the Mining Company, or some other business that stages a memorable event for the kids—and often throws in the cake for free.[10]

Since its inception, the "Experience Economy" has come full circle. Now the experience is to do it yourself. The yeast of *DIY* economics has risen in almost every industry offering youtube step-by-step motivation and guidance from *HGTV* in the comfort of your own home. We are all suckers for the next best thing that someone else is conjuring up!

There are some trends for simplicity and uncluttering. Could it be that we are tired of being duped? Could it be a shift to transforming culture rather than just consuming it? The future will tell if the next generation will *Buy It or Sell It*.

If the dead are not raised, "Let us eat and drink, for tomorrow we die."
1 Cor. 15:32

For all that is in the world—the desires of the flesh and the desires of the eyes and pride of life— is not from the Father but is from the world.
1 John 2:16

Her parents were shaped by the Depression Era and had to cobble a life together. She made it her purpose to never just get by. She studied hard to get ahead and married well, so she could have it all. She drives the latest 7-series and her kids have all the iGadgets. They live in a 5,000 sq. ft. McMansion with twice as many bathrooms as people. Chasing after the Joneses is her way of exercising, along with her new Peloton stationary. Behind the scenes though she doesn't know what to do with all the debt and anxiety except to drink and take a prescription to sleep at night.

He was a typical college student living for the party and trying to keep up his grades. He admittedly slept around without any real sense of commitment. All his frat brothers egged him on in his escapades. He didn't think much about the consequences until his rendezvous last month came knocking on his door. She was pregnant. Not wanting to step up to the plate, he convinced her that the best thing for them both was for her to get an abortion. He scrounged up the money from his friends. His life was back to normal. Little did he know that his decision would haunt him for the rest of his life.

Sloth

> We live in a world full of males who have prolonged their adolescence. They are neither boys nor men. They live, suspended as it were, between childhood and adulthood, between growing up and being grown-ups. Let's call this kind of male *Ban*, a hybrid of both boy and man. Ban is juvenile because there has been an entire niche created for him to live in the lusts of his youth. The accompanying culture not only tolerates this behavior but encourages it and endorses it.
>
> —Darrin Patrick, *Church Planter*

In ignorance, they resist any sense of responsibility for others or this world. They do not see the value in helping someone else and live as slugs toward God and others. It's difficult to get them excited about anything because nothing is worth exerting the energy, so they settle for entertainment.

Os Guinness writes:

> Sloth, the fourth of the seven deadly sins, is today the most misunderstood of all—which is ironic because, properly understood, it is the characteristically modern sin. For a start, sloth must be distinguished from

idling, a state of carefree lingering that can be admirable, as in friends lingering over a meal. But sloth must also be distinguished from the modern notion of couch-potato lethargy. Sloth is more than indolence and physical laziness. In fact, it can reveal itself in frenetic activism as easily as in lethargy because its roots are spiritual rather than physical. It is a condition of explicitly spiritual dejection that has given up in the pursuit of God, the true, the good, and the beautiful. Sloth is inner despair at the worthwhileness of the worthwhile that finally slumps into an attitude of "Who cares?"[11]

In *Hit List*, Brian Hedges offers four characteristics of sloth: 1) carelessness, 2) unwillingness to act, 3) half-hearted effort, and 4) becoming easily discouraged by any possible difficulty.[12] The sloth, if asked to serve, almost has to be dragged out of his stupor and must be constantly prodded to keep at it. When the going gets tough, they retreat into the recliner.

How long will you lie there, O sluggard? When will you arise from your sleep? A little sleep, a little slumber, a little folding of the hands to rest, and poverty will come upon you like a robber, and want like an armed man.
Prov. 6:9–11

Slothfulness casts into a deep sleep, and an idle person will suffer hunger.
Prov. 19:15

A junior in high school has spent most of his time living in the virtual world of Mortal Kombat, Assassins Creed, and Grand Theft Auto. He ignores the promptings of his mom to get out and do something mean- ingful, to get a job, to make some friends, or to go serve with the youth group. He keeps clicking away online in the gaming world with Dota, League of Legends, and Counter-Strike. His game rankings matter more than his grades or serving Mr. Stephens, the wheelchair-bound veteran down the street. Who cares anyway? He doesn't have a vision for college or a career. There will be time enough for all that later.

Stephen had been laid off again for the third time. A friend hooked him up this time with a lawn mainte- nance crew. Initially, he tried to make a good impression. After the scowls and strong words from the rest of the crew, he settled into a sloth's pace like everyone else. "Take it easy man, unless the owner is around. We don't get paid by the job but by the hour. Slow and steady." Like the previous jobs, he moved on to another one that was less strenuous. He didn't worry.

At twenty-five, he had a roof over his head and food for his belly, compliments of his parents.

---

1. Anne Lamont, *Help, Thanks, Wow: The Three Essential Prayers* (New York: Riverhead Books, 2012), 86.
2. Richard Keyes, "The Idol Factory" in *No God but God*, Os Guinness & John Seel (Chicago: Moody Press, 1992), 30–33.
3. Kelly Minter, *No Other Gods: Confronting Our Modern-Day Idols* (Ontario: David C. Cook, 2008), 17–18.
4. Sammy Rhodes, *This is Awkward: How Life's Uncomfortable Moments Open the Door to Intimacy and Connection* (Nashville: Thomas Nelson, 2016), 169.
5. Henri J. M. Nouwen, *The Return of the Prodigal Son: A Story of Homecoming* (New York: Doubleday, 1992), 52.
6. Jean M. Twenge, *Generation Me: Why Today's Young Americans Are More Confident, Assertive, Entitled—And More Miserable Than Ever Before* (New York: Simon & Schuster, Inc., 2013), 115.
7. Brené Brown, *Braving the Wilderness: The Quest for True Belonging* (New York: Random House, 2017), 56.
8. Mike Yankoski, *Under the Overpass: A Journey of Faith on the Streets of America* (Sisters: Multnomah Publishers Inc., 2005), 65.
9. Alison Stewart, *Junk: Digging Through America's Love Affair with Stuff* (Illinois: Chicago Review Press, 2016), xviii-xix.
10. B. Joseph Pine II and James H. Gilmore, "Welcome to the Experience Economy," Harvard Review, July-August 1998, https://hbr.org/1998/07/welcome-to-the-experience-economy.
11. Os Guinness, *The Call: Finding and Fulfilling God's Purpose for Your Life* (Nashville: Thomas Nelson Publishing, 2018), 194.
12. Brian G. Hedges, *Hit List: Taking Aim at the Seven Deadly Sins* (Minneapolis: Cruciform, 2014), 63.

OUR IDENTITY IN ARROGANCE

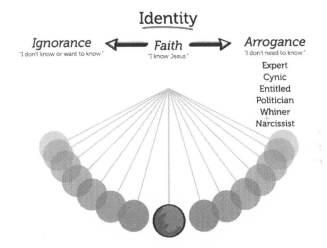

Identity

Ignorance   ⟵   *Faith*   ⟶   Arrogance

"I don't know or want to know"   "I know Jesus."   "I don't need to know"

Expert
Cynic
Entitled
Politician
Whiner
Narcissist

When thinking about arrogance, my mind first wanders to Sheldon Cooper on *The Big Bang Theory*. Then I get to Kanye West, who once said, "I am the number one most impactful artist of our generation."

Not surprisingly, I didn't think of myself. The blindspot of arrogance is that we can easily see it in others but rarely in ourselves. Arrogance enthrones our egos and makes everyone else subservient, even God. We become self-proclaimed experts, cynics, entitled, politicians, whiners, and narcissists. In this chapter, we will look at how arrogance contorts our identity.

Expert

In arrogance, experts think they know it all and have no need of others' help.

They pride themselves in their knowledge and rarely listen because they are too eager to hear themselves talk. No need for what God has to say either. They are enlightened beyond archaic religious thought. Christians are not exempt of the tendency toward hubris of an expert. Charlie Peacock warns us:

> Instead of a my-way-or-the-highway attitude, perhaps Christians could communicate something like this: We're sure of some things, so we speak with certainty about those things. But there's a lot we're not sure of, so we're trying not to speak with certainty about those things. Please forgive us when we confuse the two. In fact, that's one of the things we're certain about: We get confused, make errors, and sin against God by claiming to know things we don't.[1]

There are many dangers with the expert mindset in the workplace. One of the greatest is your need to protect your status at all costs. Robert Chen, a Fortune 500 executive coach, notes:

> When you see yourself as an expert, more energy is spent protecting this status. In the words of Carol Dweck, a renowned psychology professor focused on motivation, you shift from a growth mindset to a fixed mindset because you believed you've "made it." There isn't any more room to grow after you reach the top. Now, it's all about protecting your identity as an expert.[2]

The gravest danger is becoming an expert on God. We think we have heard it all and are experts in faith. Instead of growing in our knowledge of God, we dismiss the notion that faith has any value in our enlightened mind. The danger is not only for the non-Christian but for the Christian as well, especially ones who have grown up in the church all their lives. They may know the Scripture but have no clue what it means to have a relationship with God. They can spout out doctrine but have no sense of discipleship.

> *Woe to those who are wise in their own eyes, and shrewd in their own sight!*
> Is. 5:21

> *The Pharisee, standing by himself, prayed thus: 'God, I thank you that I am not like other men, extortioners, unjust, adulterers, or even like this tax collector. I fast twice a week; I give tithes of all that I get.*

Luke 18:11–13

Where is the one who is wise? Where is the scribe? Where is the debater of this age? Has not God made foolish the wisdom of the world? For since, in the wisdom of God, the world did not know God through wisdom, it pleased God through the folly of what we preach to save those who believe.
1 Cor. 1:20–21

———

Rosaria Butterfield shares her expert mindset before the Lord radically changed her life through a friendship with a pastor and his wife:

> The word Jesus stuck in my throat like an elephant tusk; no matter how hard I choked, I couldn't hack it out. Those who professed the name commanded my pity and wrath. As a university professor, I tired of students who seemed to believe that "knowing Jesus" meant knowing little else. Christians in particular were bad readers, always seizing opportunities to insert a Bible verse into a conversation with the same point as a punctuation mark: to end it rather than deepen it. Stupid. Pointless. Menacing. That's what I thought of Christians and their god Jesus, who in paintings looked as powerful as a Breck Shampoo commercial model.[3]

My friend is a man's man who claims to be a self-made man. He's done pretty well when it comes to putting food on the table and a stable bank account. He has learned most things by the school of hard knocks. He doesn't have much patience with academic types, and church is pretty much a waste of time. He's been there and done that when it comes to most things and doesn't take correction too kindly. The real world is his teacher and not some religion. He scoffs under his breath, "They're all a bunch of idiots and fanatics with soft hands."

Cynic

Cynicism begins with the wry assurance that everyone has an angle. Behind every silver lining is a cloud. The cynic is always observing, critiquing, but never engaged, loving, and hoping... to be cynical is to be distant. While offering a false intimacy of being "in the know," cynicism actually destroys intimacy. It leads to a creeping bitterness that can deaden and even destroy the spirit.

Most of us do not actively seek to embrace cynicism. We fall into it. Cynicism often arises from painful disillusionment when the veil is torn off disillusionment—when the rug gets violently jerked out from under us, when the wool long pulled over our eyes is yanked off. The moment of the defining injury is often abrupt, having the effect of an explosive collision that tosses us into a pit.

—Paul Miller, *A Praying Life*

Cynicism ignites an angry pride in us. We're declaring that we will never be duped again. In arrogance, a cynic begins to doubt most everything, especially God or anything dealing with faith. Nothing is worth putting your full trust in because it will fail you. The observable is master since it can be proven scientifically and controlled. Cynics think they are mastered by no one, but little do they know that they are mastered by their own pride.

> *Now Thomas, one of the twelve, called the Twin, was not with them when Jesus came. So the other disciples told him, "We have seen the Lord." But he said to them, "Unless I see in his hands the mark of the nails, and place my finger into the mark of the nails, and place my hand into his side, I will never believe.*
> John 20:24–25

> *Philip found Nathanael and said to him, "We have found him of whom Moses in the Law and also the prophets wrote, Jesus of Nazareth, the son of Joseph." Nathanael said to him, "Can anything good come out of Nazareth?" Philip said to him, "Come and see."*

John 1:45–46

She grew up in a well-educated home. Her mom had a PhD and her dad a Masters degree in engineering. She prides herself on not being ignorant and being good at assimi-lating facts. She is following in her mother's footsteps by graduating summa cum laude from college. She belittled her roommate because she was attending a campus ministry and going to a small group Bible study. She mocked her for wasting her time with those hypocrites. Religion was for the gullible. She would never get hurt by them again. Her cynicism wasn't so much fueled by her intellect as much as it was from the wound of being rejected back in high school from two popular Christian classmates. She closed her heart off then and wasn't about to open it again.

My friend is a young woman who was taught to be cynical about God, especially Jesus. When she was a toddler, her older brother was sick, and her mother went to various reli-gions to heal him. Finally, she asked Jesus to heal him. Shortly afterwards, he died. Her mom could never forgive Jesus for not saving her son, and she exuded this anger and disappointment onto her daughter. A mutual friend began meeting with her twenty years later and is listening to the questions of her heart and sharing the love of Christ. By God's grace, she is growing in faith.

Entitled

> *Entitlement* is perhaps the top word associated with the Millennial generation. In fact, 71 percent of American adults think of Millennials as "selfish," and 65 percent think Millennials are "entitled." Whether or not you believe the "entitlement" label is accurate, perception is reality. Unaddressed entitlement in your Millennial workers can result in unethical behaviors, higher turnover, underperformance, lower job satisfaction, and/or loss of leadership influence, as Millennials might view their managers as unreasonable, hard-headed, or irrelevant.
> —Ryan Jenkins, "Why Millennials Are So Entitled (Parents Are Partly Blamed)"

Millennials' entitlement is not due to being coddled and overprotected like Gen Z. It is actually "an adaptation to a world of abundance."[4] With so many choices, the world is their oyster.

The entitled heart is centered on the belief that God owes them the good life. They think highly of themselves and assume everyone should love them since they are so lovable. They deserve to be blessed because they are such a blessing. Sometimes this mentality is brought on because they were initially dealt a bad hand (race, poverty, disability, gender, broken family). The entitled believe their privileges are their God-given rights. They tend to blame others and shirk their own personal culpability or responsibility. They expect others to do for them whether it be parents, friends, employers, or the government. The entitled may fight for others as long as they can share in the benefits. If the effort outweighs the benefit, the entitled tend to lose interest, and they think it is not worth their time and energy to continue. They are takers rather than givers.

When things don't go their way, they immediately think there is something wrong outside of themselves. God is usually the culprit, and he ought to be loving them much better.

> Then the mother of the sons of Zebedee came up to him
> with her sons, and kneeling before him she asked him for
> something. And he said to her, "What do you want?"
> She said to him, "Say that these two sons of mine are to
> sit, one at your right hand and one at your left, in your
> kingdom." Jesus answered, "You do not know what you
> are asking. Are you able to drink the cup that I am to
> drink?" They said to him, "We are able."
> Matthew 20:20–22

> Now his older son was in the field, and as he came and
> drew near to the house, he heard music and dancing. And
> he called one of the servants and asked what these things

meant. And he said to him, 'Your brother has come, and your father has killed the fattened calf, because he has received him back safe and sound.' But he was angry and refused to go in. His father came out and entreated him, but he answered his father, 'Look, these many years I have served you, and I never disobeyed your command, yet you never gave me a young goat, that I might celebrate with my friends. But when this son of yours came, who has devoured your property with prostitutes, you killed the fattened calf for him!' And he said to him, 'Son, you are always with me, and all that is mine is yours. It was fitting to celebrate and be glad, for this your brother was dead, and is alive; he was lost, and is found.

Luke 15:25–32

———

Since I was born with Spina Bifida, I grew up with an entitlement mentality. I have to fight it almost every day. I think God owes me a good life since he dealt me a bad hand from the beginning. I had and continue to have a high view of myself, despite my disabilities. I expect others to initially think highly of me. I don't doubt God's love for me because he is blessed to have me as his child, and he owes me.

———

Government housing and assistance create a perfect storm of entitlement. Many of the women start out trying to make it through other means, but hopelessness and frustration set in. Without the father around to help feed the little ones, they settle into a life of government assistance. To make the leap vocationally and economically doesn't make sense when their government benefits, housing, and food stamps account for much more. After a while most get stuck, perpetuating generational dependence and a passive aggressive entitlement.

My friend, a business owner and a fellow pastor, sought to remedy this trap by starting a job training program initially called Jobs Partnership and is now a global ministry called Jobs for Life. This ministry brought together business owners, who needed good workers, the under-employed, who needed a job with benefits that surpassed government assistance, and mentors, who wanted to break the cycle of poverty. Jobs for Life gives gospel hope in the realm of vocation and dignity. Its strength is the relationships it builds throughout the journey and the conversations along the way.

Politician

In arrogance, the politician builds a network of admirers and uses them to gain privilege, position, or pleasure. They manipulate others to get what they want and will move on quickly if the benefits of the relationship are not bearing fruit. The politician may have many constituents but very few neighbors that are true friends. Politicians are manipulators.

The manipulator deliberately creates an imbalance of power and exploits the victim to serve his or her agenda. Most manipulative individuals have four common characteristics:

> They know how to detect your weaknesses.
> Once found, they use your weaknesses against you.
> Through their shrewd machinations, they convince you to give up something of yourself in order to serve their self-centered interests.
> In work, social, and family situations, once a manipulator succeeds in taking advantage of you, he or she will likely repeat the violation until you put a stop to the exploitation.[5]

In his book *Death by Suburbs*, David Goetz challenges what the ulterior motives are for our friendships. He writes:

> You can't use relationships as a means to position yourself in life and then also expect to experience in them the kind of friendship that sweetens life and takes the edge off its hard parts. Obviously, most, if not all, relationships have transactional traces to them. I gain from friendship, I give in friendship. Yet true friendship is one of the great gifts of the thicker

life and subverts the politics of community in suburbia.[6]

I think the hardest betrayal is when it comes from an assumed friend who has used us for their own selfish ends.

He said also to the man who had invited him, "When you give a dinner or a banquet, do not invite your friends or your brothers or your relatives or rich neighbors, lest they also invite you in return and you be repaid. But when you give a feast, invite the poor, the crippled, the lame, the blind, and you will be blessed, because they cannot repay you. For you will be repaid at the resurrection of the just."
Luke 14:12–14

While he was still speaking, Judas came, one of the twelve, and with him a great crowd with swords and clubs, from the chief priests and the elders of the people. Now the betrayer had given them a sign, saying, "The one I will kiss is the man; seize him." And he came up to Jesus at once and said, "Greetings, Rabbi!" And he kissed him. Jesus said to him, "Friend, do what you came to do." Then they came up and laid hands on Jesus and seized him.
Matt. 26:47–50

———

A young professional friend of mine had run through

several relationships during college but none of them lasted. She put so much pressure on the men to meet her needs. She found her identity on their arm. She expected them to do her bidding. After hesitating, she joined the online dating world. This way she could ensure getting the perfect match. She wanted someone to complete her. One after another, her heart would open up but then be crushed. No one ever could satisfy her longing to be whole.

———

A friend of mine got on staff with a parachurch organization. I was excited to have him come to our church and partner in the gospel ministry. He informed me that the ministry leaders didn't encourage him to attend a smaller church. He needed to be in a big church so it and its members could sponsor the ministry.

Whiner

In arrogance, the whiner complains about almost everything but is unwilling to do anything about it. They make judgments on culture with limited knowledge. They question even if something truly good does take place because they like whining about something.

Americans have mastered the art of whining. Complaining has become habit. Streeter Seidell humorously pontificates:

> So what is a White Whine? There are infinite shades of gray when it comes to classifying the various types of White Whine, but at their core they're just First-World Problems. That is the notion that no matter how good you have it—drinking coconut water, eating at fancy restaurants, having an iPhone, being able to afford childcare—you're still annoyed. That is the common denominator in all White Whines. To be a White Whiner your complaint must convey, simultaneously, that you are both fortunate and irritated.[7]

According to The Gallup Organization, "Negativity costs the U.S. economy $250–$300 billion in lost productivity each year and Truejobs.com says the # 1 cause of office stress is coworkers and their complaining."[8] Many have called Whiners "Energy Vampires" because they suck the life out of any endeavor and divert so much energy away from the task at hand. Whiners waste everyone's time without offering help or a solution to the obstacles that are being faced. Instead of transforming culture, they are too busy creating a culture of "Wha... Whaa... Whaaa... Woe Is Me!"

> *And the people complained in the hearing of the LORD about their misfortunes, and when the LORD heard it, his anger was kindled, and the fire of the LORD burned among them and consumed some outlying parts of the*

camp. Then the people cried out to Moses, and Moses prayed to the LORD, and the fire died down. So the name of that place was called Taberah, because the fire of the LORD burned among them. Now the rabble that was among them had a strong craving. And the people of Israel also wept again and said, "Oh that we had meat to eat! We remember the fish we ate in Egypt that cost nothing, the cucumbers, the melons, the leeks, the onions, and the garlic. But now our strength is dried up, and there is nothing at all but this manna to look at."
Num. 11:1–6

———

A very intelligent young man worked hard all through high school and prided himself in his grades. He did excellent on the SAT and applied to all the top schools. He got accepted to great universities but was denied acceptance in his prized first-choice Ivy-League school. He pouted and stomped for months. He whined all through the summer until heading off to college on a full scholarship. What a travesty!

———

I encounter a lot of whining in marriage counseling. There are many areas that need to be address, but what hurts the marriage the most is when one spouse goes on and on whining about how the other spouse has made a mess of the relationship. At best, the whiner may admit to his or her own few small mistakes. The whiner is confident that the marriage will be saved only if the other spouse changes.

Narcissist

Narcissism has come a long way since the Greek myth, where Narcissus rejected the advances of the nymph Echo causing him to fall in love with his own reflection in a pool of water. Instead of being enamored with their own self-image, modern narcissists set out to destroy all those who do not cater to their every whim.

In arrogance, narcissists only think about themselves. It is all about their own glory and well-being. Others exist to laud and serve them. It is beneath them to roll up their sleeves and serve someone else. They will not relinquish their power that way. If they do serve others, it will be held over them as a favor to be returned later. In a book on this subject, Jean Twenge and Keith Campbell write:

> In fact, narcissism causes almost all of the things that Americans hoped high self-esteem would prevent, including aggression, materialism, lack of caring for others, and shallow values. In trying to build a society that celebrates high self-esteem, self-expression, and "loving yourself," Americans have inadvertently

created more narcissists—and a culture that brings out the narcissistic behavior in all of us.[9]

I am afraid America has gone from the Home of the Brave to the Haunt of the Narcissist.

Then Herod, when he saw that he had been tricked by the wise men, became furious, and he sent and killed all the male children in Bethlehem and in all that region who were two years old or under, according to the time that he had ascertained from the wise men.
Matt. 2:16

And there came out from the camp of the Philistines a champion named Goliath of Gath, whose height was six cubits and a span. He had a helmet of bronze on his head, and he was armed with a coat of mail, and the weight of the coat was five thousand shekels of bronze. And he had bronze armor on his legs, and a javelin of bronze slung between his shoulders. The shaft of his spear was like a weaver's beam, and his spear's head weighed six hundred shekels of iron. And his shield-bearer went before him. He stood and shouted to the ranks of Israel, "Why have you come out to draw up for battle? Am I not a Philistine, and are you not servants of Saul? Choose a man for yourselves, and let him come down to me. If he is able to fight with me and kill me, then we will be your servants. But if I prevail against him and kill him, then you shall be our servants and serve us."
1 Sam. 17:4–9

———

After the initial shame of getting caught in an affair, he quickly turned to blame-shifting. It was all her fault. If she had loved me the way I needed her to love me, and if she hadn't given priority to their child, I wouldn't have been driven into another woman's arms. As the marriage crumbled and the legal proceedings moved forward, his heart hardened against his wife. He did everything to make her suffer and wish she had never defied him.

———

My friend was a very successful and well-known pastor, author, and speaker. His leadership skills were rare and everyone was drawn to his charisma. Like many other mega-church pastors, his celebrity led to his downfall. He began to think too highly of himself, and his ministry became more about him than the Lord. He became domineering and controlling. He verbally abused his team and crossed the line on more than one occasion. Narcissism inflates the ego until it pops in a million pieces.

Conclusion

I know that was a lot to take in so quickly, but you will get more proficient with the terminology as you watch, listen, and share Questions of the Heart conversations. Remember to be careful not to start making assumptions and stereotyping your friends. Spend time in prayer and the Scriptures to grow in your relationship with the Lord, so you can be the friend that your friends need. Let your conversations be seasoned with grace and love your friends well, even the whiners and narcissists.

With the terminology in hand, I now want to walk you through the Questions of the Heart conversation. Remember it's not a canned evangelism technique, so the conversation isn't set in stone and usually takes a turn here and there along the way. It does help though to have this basic conversation guide as a foundation. Hopefully it will give you the breadcrumbs to guide you into meaningful Gospel opportunities.

---

1. Charlie Peacock, *New Way to Be Human: A Provocative Look at What It Means to Follow Jesus* (Colorado: Waterbrook Press, 2004), 12.

2. Robert Chen, "The Downside of Being an Expert," lifehack.org, accessed 2020, https:// www.lifehack.org/299242/the-downside-being-expert.

3. Rosaria Champagne Butterfield, "My Train Wreck Conversion: As a Leftist Lesbian Professor, I despised Christians. Then I Somehow Became One," christianitytoday.com, February 7, 2013, https://www.christianitytoday.com/ct/2013/january-february/my-train-wreck-conversion.html.

4. Joel Stein, "Millennials: The Me Me Me Generation: Millennials are lazy, entitled narcissists who still live with their parents, Why they'll save us all," Time.com, May 20, 2013, https://time.com/247/ millennials-the-me-me-me-generation/.

5. Preston Ni M.S.B.A., "How to Recognize and Handle Manipulative Relationships:

Most manipulators have traits in common," psychologytoday.com, July 13, 2014, https://
www.psychologytoday.com/us/blog/communication-success/201407/how-recognize-and-handle-   manipulative-relationships.

6. David L. Goetz, *Death by Suburb: How to Keep the Suburbs from Killing Your Soul* (New York: HarperCollins Publisher, 2006) 154–155.

7. Streeter Seidell, *White Whine: A Study ff First-World Problems* (Massachusetts: Adams Media, 2013), 12.

8. "Stop the Complaining to Save Your Company Culture," spotio.com, October 24, 2017, https:// spotio.com/blog/stop-the-complaining-to-save-your-company-culture/.

9. Jean M. Twenge, PhD and W. Keith Campbell, PhD, *The Narcissism Epidemic*

THE CONVERSATION

> What if you met a saint on the road, and that
> saint had a map and had spent time at every stop-
> off that lured but then disappointed you? What if
> he'd already met the "you" you somehow want to
> be? What if he could introduce you to the person
> you've been looking for and lead you to a house
> with many rooms, where a Friend would open
> the door and say, "Welcome home. You can rest
> here"?
> —James K. A. Smith, *On the Road with Saint
> Augustine*

When I am in a conversation with someone, and life
begins to be shared with each other (challenges, missed
opportunities, decisions, suffering, relationships,
finances, spirituality), I listen for where his or her identity is being challenged or if it's in a full-blown crisis.

I respond with something like, "At moments like

these, I find that my identity can be challenged. How would you say this is challenging who you are?"

As I've said, people don't like to think they are in an identity crisis, so I leave it at "being challenged." Then I listen for more of the questions of their heart. Sometimes they can pinpoint where their identity is being challenged, or they ask questions for me to help them understand what I am talking about in regard to identity. Sharing a personal story and knowing the terminology section can help you explain it naturally.

As the conversation moves forward, I ask, "Can I show you something that has really helped me realign my life during these times? I think it will help explain what I am talking about."

Thanks to Dan Roam, the author of *The Back of a Napkin* and *BLAH, BLAH, BLAH,* I grab a napkin or scrap of paper, and I begin to draw the Identity Pendulum. If I am out and about, I just talk them through it, but it is more understandable if it's written out.

I write the word "identity" at the top of the napkin.

And I say something like, "We all find our identity in something or someone. It  shapes and defines who we are, our purpose, what we value, care about and how we view others and the world around us."

Identity

Learner

Worshiper

Beloved

Neighbor

Culturemaker

Servant

I then begin to write the six core identities underneath the word "identity," leaving some space in between.

I explain as I go and give a short definition of each:

Actually if you break it down, our true identity is built around our relationship toward God, others, and the world. The Bible says we were created this way by God with honor and value in his image. He shaped us to be Learners, Worshipers, Beloved, Neighbors, Culturemakers, and Servants.

As a Learner, we were created with an ability to reason, to discover, and to formulate a worldview—an understanding about life.

As a Worshiper, we were created with a desire for adoration, praise, and thanksgiving—to worship with all of who we are. The one whom we think about most, feel most intensely about, and our behavior is most influenced by, is the one we worship. We give that person or thing the most weight (glory) in our lives.

As the Beloved, we were created to be loved and to love with all our heart, mind, soul, and strength. We long for acceptance and approval—to know and to be known.

As a Neighbor, we are created to live in community, to be generous, and to enjoy all the good things that we have been given with others. We are shaped for family and friendship.

As a Culturemaker, we are created with gifts, passions and creativity to bless, and shape the culture around us. We live for our purpose and to make a difference.

As a Servant, we are created to care for others and to bless others. To not only think about ourselves but to put others before our own interests. We are called to enter into the brokenness of life in order to bring wholeness. We are to bring light into darkness and to pick up the pieces to make something beautiful.

At this point I ask if they are tracking with me. I listen for more questions of the heart. I then ask, "In light of what is going on in your life, which identity or identities are being challenged right now?"

I let a minute pass, and I pray silently that the Lord

would open up this heart for the Gospel, so that the pressing heart question is brought to the forefront. At this time the identity crisis is put on the table. When one or two of the identities are chosen, I circle them and listen after I ask, "Why those identities?"

This usually opens up the conversation with their back-story and other factors connected with what is going on. I then draw the word "faith" underneath the word "identity" and above the six core identities and circle it.

Identity

(Faith)

Learner

Worshiper

Beloved

Neighbor

Culturemaker

Servant

And I say something like:

Since God designed us this way, we must trust him by faith according to what he says is true about our identity. By faith, I put my trust in what God says about me in the Bible rather than anything else, even my own heart. In doing so, I grow to understand who I was created to be—my true identity. By faith, I follow God's lead as I figure out life, and how I fit into the big picture. I can wake up every morning trusting by faith that my life is in alignment with God. But my faith constantly gets challenged. The Bible calls this temptation, which leads to sin, a decision to rebel against God. The root of this is pride. Pride looks different in all of us, but it has two main postures—the postures of ignorance and arrogance.

I then write "ignorance" on the left side of the word "faith" and "arrogance" on the right. I explain what both mean.

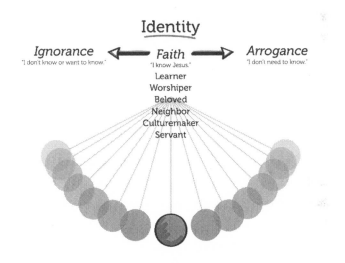

I begin drawing the pendulum arm swinging from side to side, and I say something like:

If we are honest, by nature we choose to take matters into our own hands—to set our own agenda. We choose to ignore what God says or arrogantly think we know better. In doing so, we try to find our identity in a lot of different things, which were never supposed to define us. As we put our identity in the hands of anything other than God (a philosophy, a position, a pleasure, a person, a purpose, a power), our identity swings away from what God has intended. Actually, we were all born out of alignment with God, and in that state we continue to choose ignorance and arrogance—to go our own way. Our lives get out of alignment and ultimately swing into an identity crisis because these things will always let us down. By giving them ultimate value in our lives, they further our separation from God and lead us down a destructive path. We are left with shame, guilt, regret, and disappointment.

Then I will ask, "What would you say is your posture toward God in your challenge right now? Ignorance or arrogance?"

Listen closely to the explanation about the posture of ignorance or arrogance. This will reveal a predominant posture toward God and open the door to explaining how Jesus dealt with people with a similar posture of ignorance and arrogance.

I then say something like:

Thanks for being honest. None of us want to admit that we are ignorant or arrogant. Actually, the first humans on earth tried to cover up their ignorance and arrogance by shifting the blame to each other. We tend to do the same and follow in their footsteps. Arrogance and ignorance distort our true identity, and we become someone we never intended to be.

Identity

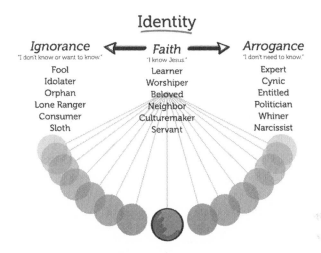

Ignorance
"I don't know or want to know."

Faith
"I know Jesus."

Arrogance
"I don't need to know."

Ignorance	Faith	Arrogance
Fool	Learner	Expert
Idolater	Worshiper	Cynic
Orphan	Beloved	Entitled
Lone Ranger	Neighbor	Politician
Consumer	Culturemaker	Whiner
Sloth	Servant	Narcissist

I then begin to draw the distorted identities and circle their specific ones shaped by the posture of ignorance or arrogance.

Depending on time, I either go through all of the identity crises, or I just focus on the one or two that have been selected. I might say:

> In regard to our identity as a Learner, ignorance makes us a Fool without any regard to truth, or in arrogance we become a self-proclaimed Expert thinking we know it all and exchange the truth of God for a lie.

> In regard to our identity as a Worshiper, ignorance makes us an Idolator, where we worship the created rather than the Creator. Or in arrogance we become a Cynic questioning everything and denying that God even exists.

In regard to our identity as the Beloved, ignorance makes us live as Orphans depressed as if no one cares about us, or in arrogance we become the Entitled, demanding the good life with everyone owing us love.

In regard to our identity as a Neighbor, ignorance makes us a Loner isolating ourselves and withdrawing from community, or in arrogance we become a Politician using and manipulating everyone to get what we want.

In regard to our identity as a Culturemaker, ignorance makes us a Consumer allowing the world to try and satisfy us, or in arrogance we become a Whiner complaining about everything not willing to make a difference to change the culture.

In regard to our identity as a Servant, ignorance makes us a Sloth apathetic about exerting any energy to care about others, or in arrogance we become a Narcissist demanding everyone serve us.

I then say something like, "Being labeled is not enjoyable, but sometimes it's good to take a good look in the mirror and see where our identity is in crisis. In light of what we have talked about, what questions are rising out of your heart?"

I then listen, help answer their questions, and end our time with:

I'm glad for us that God loves both the ignorant and the arrogant. The Bible shares a lot about how God engaged people facing identity challenges and those in full-blown identity crisis. He gives insight and hope to the ignorant and humbles the arrogant so they can see their need and find new life. The crux of the Bible is that God loved us so much that he left heaven and entered into the crisis of humanity as a man himself. Jesus is called Emmanuel, which means, "God with Us."

How comforting to know that Jesus came to be with us in the midst of our crisis. He not only came to be with us. He took on our sinful identity and bore the penalty and consequence of our ignorance and arrogance, which leads to destruction and death in our thinking, relationships, and vocations—in all the areas of this life and in the life to come.

Jesus became the Savior and Substitute for those who live by faith in him. He shared in our identity so that we could share in his identity now and forevermore by faith through grace. Jesus, our Lord and Savior, fulfills all these identities as Truth, God, Love, God Incarnate, Creator, and Divine Servant.

I know I talked way too much, but I hope it has been helpful. Thanks for entrusting me with the challenge you are going through. I really count it a privilege to have you in my life. Know that I will be praying for you. If you would like to get together some more to talk, I'd love to be an encouragement. We could look at a story or two about how Jesus walked with someone in similar identity challenges.

This is the Come & See Principle. Jesus used this principle often. He would challenge someone and then ask them to come and follow him. Jesus was entrusting the person to the Holy Spirit to draw them further into a relationship with him. Remember our Father is sovereign, and no one comes to Jesus unless he draws and calls them to himself.

And he said to them, "Follow me, and I will make you fishers of men." Immediately they left their nets and followed him.
Matt. 4:19–20

And Jesus said to him, "Follow me, and leave the dead to bury their own dead." Matt. 8:22

As Jesus passed on from there, he saw a man called Matthew sitting at the tax booth, and he said to him, "Follow me." And he rose and followed him.
Matt. 9:9

Then Jesus told his disciples, "If anyone would come after me, let him deny himself and take up his cross and follow me. For whoever would save his life will lose it, but whoever loses his life for my sake will find it."
Matt. 16:25

Depending on what the person says, I try to set the next conversation up for the next week (See Follow-up Conversations). If you feel comfortable and think it's appropriate, ask if you can say a short prayer. I usually send a follow-up text the next day to see how he or she is doing and confirm the next meeting. I lift this person up to the Lord throughout the week and ask God to do immeasurably more than I can ask or think.

Now to him who is able to do far more abundantly than all that we ask or think, according to the power at work within us, to him be glory in the church and in Christ Jesus throughout all generations, forever and ever. Amen.
Eph. 3:20–21

OUR IDENTITY IN CHRIST

A man once said to a pastor that he would be happy to believe in Christianity if the cleric could give him a watertight argument for its truth. The pastor replied, "What if God hasn't given us a watertight argument, but rather a watertight person?"… Ultimately faith and certainty grow as we get to know more about Jesus, who he is, and what he did.

—Tim Keller, *The Reason for God*

Each identity finds its fulfillment in the Lordship of Christ. Each identity reveals the beauty of who Jesus Christ is and the work that he has accomplished for his people. By grace through faith, Christ is transforming us by the Spirit into the very image of Christ. The ultimate goal of *Questions of the Heart* is that our friends might behold Jesus, the One True Living God, in whom they can find their true identity. Along the way in your conversations, the hope is that they will come to grips that Jesus our Lord and Savior is the Way, Truth, Love, God Incarnate, Creator, and Divine Servant—the fulfillment of their specific crisis and every need of the heart.

> *And we all, with unveiled face, beholding the glory of the Lord, are being transformed into the same image from one degree of glory to another. For this comes from the Lord who is the Spirit.*
> 2 Cor. 3:18

Jesus is Truth—Learner

In the gospel of John, Pilate arrogantly asked Jesus, "What is truth?" Pilate didn't realize that he was looking right in the face of Truth himself. A more brilliant, insightful question would have been, "Are you the truth?"

In the letter of Hebrews, it says God spoke through many different ways in the past, but his final word is through his Son. Jesus declared, *"I am the way, the truth and the life"* (John 14:6).

Most religions offer a way, a philosophy to live by. But Jesus offers himself. It is through his life, death, and resurrection that salvation is offered. It's where we find our true identity. Without his grace and the gift of the Holy Spirit, we can't comprehend him as Truth nor can we follow his teachings. When we come to him as a learner, the scales fall from our eyes, and we can see him for who he truly is. The Scriptures come alive in our hearts and begin to speak to the inmost parts of our soul.

When Jesus was sharing about his death to the crowds, they began turning away because the teachings were difficult. He asked his disciples if they were going to leave as well. Simon Peter answered him, *"Lord, to whom shall we go? You have the words of eternal life"* (John 6:68). As a disciple, we follow Jesus not merely as a great teacher but as the one who offers eternal life. He is the God of truth—Truth himself.

Jesus Is the Word

In the beginning was the Word, and the Word was with God, and the Word was God. He was in the beginning with God. All things were made through him, and without him was not anything made that was made. In him was life, and the life was the light of men. The light shines in the darkness, and the darkness has not overcome it.... And the Word became flesh and dwelt among us, and we have seen his glory, glory as of the only Son from the Father, full of grace and truth.
John 1:1–5,14

Jesus Is the Way, the Truth, and the Life

Jesus said to him, "I am the way, and the truth, and the life. No one comes to the Father except through me. If you had known me, you would have known my Father also. From now on you do know him and have seen him."
John 14:6–7

Jesus Upholds the World by His Word

*Long ago, at many times and in many ways, God spoke
to our fathers by the prophets, but in these last days he
has spoken to us by his Son, whom he appointed the heir
of all things, through whom also he created the world.
He is the radiance of the glory of God and the exact
imprint of his nature, and he upholds the universe by the
word of his power.*

Heb. 1:1–3

Jesus Is God—Worshiper

Most people will at least admit that
Jesus was a good or even a great
man, but they are not willing to
declare that he is God. The Scriptures on the other hand don't allow
for such a limited description of
him. They proclaim that Jesus is none other than God
himself. His disciples were in awe that even the waves
and wind obeyed him. The Pharisees called him a blas-
phemer, because he claimed to forgive sin, which only
God can do. He healed the sick, gave sight to the blind,
made the lame to leap for joy, cast out demons, and
spoke with the authority of heaven.

The Scriptures declare that Jesus holds all things
together by the power of his word. He is the Only Way
of salvation, the Lord of heaven and earth and under the
earth, and the Judge of all mankind. He is the Fulfillment of all the Scriptures, the Only One Worthy of
worship and praise. He knows the intent of every man's
heart and has the power to do all things according to his

will. He and the Father are one with the Holy Spirit ruling and reigning supreme. He is the Alpha and the Omega—the Great I Am.

Jesus Is King of Kings

When they [Magi] saw the star, they rejoiced exceedingly with great joy. And going into the house, they saw the child [Jesus] with Mary his mother, and they fell down and worshiped him. Then, opening their treasures, they offered him gifts, gold and frankincense and myrrh.

Matt. 2:10–11

Jesus Is Lord over Creation

And Peter answered him, "Lord, if it is you, command me to come to you on the water." He said, "Come." So Peter got out of the boat and walked on the water and came to Jesus. But when he saw the wind, he was afraid, and beginning to sink he cried out, "Lord, save me." Jesus immediately reached out his hand and took hold of him, saying to him, "O you of little faith, why did you doubt?" And when they got into the boat, the wind ceased. And those in the boat worshiped him, saying, "Truly you are the Son of God."

Matt. 14:28–33

Jesus Is Lord over the Effects of Death

Jesus heard that they had cast him out, and having found him he said, "Do you believe in the Son of Man?" He answered, "And who is he, sir, that I may believe in him?" Jesus said to him, "You have seen him, and it is he

who is speaking to you." He said, "Lord, I believe," and
he worshiped him.
John 9:35–38

Jesus Is Love—Beloved

The Scriptures say that God is love, and he defines love by the life, death, and resurrection of Jesus Christ. He lovingly and willingly laid down his life for his enemies. He demonstrated both the justice and mercy of God on the cross as our sacrificial lamb. He became our substitute, taking the wrath we deserved and imputing to us his own righteousness. Even now he is preparing a place for us to be with him for eternity, and he intercedes at the right hand of the Father tending to our every need. Even though we are unfaithful, he remains faithful and is not ashamed to call us his brothers.

He loved the least of them, the powerful, the wealthy, the poor, the prostitute, the tax collector, the fisherman, the doctor, and the lawyer. His love was unmerited and many times unwanted, but nonetheless much needed. Every word he spoke and every deed he displayed was an expression of his love. He gave hope to the hopeless, and he humbled the mighty, so that they might enter into his love for them. This is love, not that we loved him first, but that he has loved us before the foundations of the earth. He is the embodiment of covenant love—he is Love.

Jesus Loves Us as Much as the Father Loved Him

As the Father has loved me, so have I loved you. Abide in my love.

John 15:9

Jesus Loved His Disciples to the End

Now before the Feast of the Passover, when Jesus knew that his hour had come to depart out of this world to the Father, having loved his own who were in the world, he loved them to the end.

John 13:1

Jesus Loved His Friends by Conquering Death

When Jesus saw her weeping, and the Jews who had come with her also weeping, he was deeply moved in his spirit and greatly troubled. And he said, "Where have you laid him?" They said to him, "Lord, come and see." Jesus wept. So the Jews said, "See how he loved him!"…
When he had said these things, he cried out with a loud voice, "Lazarus, come out."

John 11:33–36, 43

Jesus Is God Incarnate—Neighbor

Most people imagine God as someone who is far off, distant, and aloof. But the gospel of John describes Jesus as the Word who took on flesh and dwelt among us. God came near and introduced himself. *The Message* translation puts it this way: *"The*

Word became flesh and blood, and moved into the neighborhood" (John 1:14, The Message). Jesus wasn't like anyone else that walked on the face of the earth. He was fully man and fully God—one person with two natures.

Unlike every religion in the world where people attempt to get to God, Christianity declares that God came after people by leaving heaven and taking on flesh. He did so to identify with us and to give himself for us. He came to do what we could not do for ourselves.

He is the best neighbor in the world! He knows everything about us and still wants to be our friend. Jesus said he will never leave us nor forsake us. He found us on the side of the road broken, sinful, and shameful. He is the only one that was willing to stop, and he is the only one able to heal our physical, psychological, social, and spiritual alienation caused by our sin. He truly is the Friend of Sinners—our Emmanuel.

Jesus Moved into Our Neighborhood

And the Word became flesh and dwelt among us, and we have seen his glory, glory as of the only Son from the Father, full of grace and truth.
John 1:14

Jesus Is Our Friend

This is my commandment, that you love one another as I have loved you. Greater love has no one than this, that someone lay down his life for his friends. You are my friends if you do what I command you. No longer do I call you servants, for the servant does not know what his master is doing; but I have called you friends, for all that

I have heard from my Father I have made known to you. You did not choose me, but I chose you and appointed you that you should go and bear fruit and that your fruit should abide, so that whatever you ask the Father in my name, he may give it to you. These things I command you, so that you will love one another.
John 15:12–17

Jesus Is a Friend of Sinners
The Son of Man came eating and drinking, and they say, "Look at him! A glutton and a drunkard, a friend of tax collectors and sinners!" Yet wisdom is justified by her deeds.
Matt. 11:19

Jesus Is Creator—Culturemaker

In Colossians Paul writes, *"For by him all things were created, in heaven and on earth, visible and invisible, whether thrones or dominions or rulers or authorities—all things were created through him and for him. And he is before all things,* *and in him all things hold together"* (Col. 1:16–17). The Psalms tell us God has created each human being fearfully and wonderfully in his image. He knows the number of hairs on our head and the grains of sand on the seashore. He is the Author and Perfecter of our faith. We are his workmanship with a calling that he has prepared beforehand for us to live out and fulfill. He has placed us where we are and given us gifts, possessions, and positions to honor him in our sphere of influence.

We are to transform every aspect of this life on earth as it is in heaven. We are to be culturemakers reflecting his creativity and resourcefulness. He says we are his ambassadors, his vice-regents in the world called to declare and display his kingdom. As we follow him, we work out our salvation by applying the Gospel in our marriages, families, neighborhoods, workplaces, churches, and leisure activities. He is the great architect of his kingdom, and he is bringing his kingdom to bear on this world in us and through us.

Jesus Is Creator of All Things

For by him all things were created, in heaven and on earth, visible and invisible, whether thrones or dominions or rulers or authorities—all things were created through him and for him.

Col. 1:16

Jesus Creatively Made Us His Workmanship

For we are his workmanship, created in Christ Jesus for good works, which God prepared beforehand, that we should walk in them.

Eph. 2:10

Jesus Blesses Our Work

Therefore, my beloved brothers, be steadfast, immovable, always abounding in the work of the Lord, knowing that in the Lord your labor is not in vain.

1 Cor. 15:58

Jesus Is the Suffering Servant—Servant

Jesus came not to be served but to serve and to give his life as a ransom for many. Even though he is Lord, he came to serve his people. He washed the disciples' feet as a symbol of his undying love. This act of service foreshadows that he would wash the sin from the texture of their souls by his own shed blood. The Jewish nation wanted him to come as a conquering king to vanquish its earthly enemies, but Jesus came to conquer sin, the enemy within. He endured humiliation, insults, unwarranted mocking, and physical abuse, even death on a cross for us. He faithfully did all that the Father had sent him to do and all that we needed him to do as our Savior. He served willingly with joy in his heart. He entered into our dark places and our broken-ness to give us hope and a new life. Jesus truly is the Suffering Servant.

Jesus Is the Promised Servant of the Lord

For he grew up before him like a young plant, and like a root out of dry ground; he had no form or majesty that we should look at him, and no beauty that we should desire him. He was despised and rejected by men, a man of sorrows and acquainted with grief; and as one from whom men hide their faces he was despised, and we esteemed him not.

Surely he has borne our griefs and carried our sorrows; yet we esteemed him stricken, smitten by God, and afflicted. But he was pierced for our transgressions; he was crushed for our iniquities;

upon him was the chastisement that brought us peace, and with his wounds we are healed. All we like sheep have gone astray; we have turned—every one—to his own way; and the LORD has laid on him the iniquity of us all.
Is. 53:2–6

Jesus Is Our Ransom
For even the Son of Man came not to be served but to serve, and to give his life as a ransom for many.
Mark 10:45

Jesus Is the Great High Priest and Sacrifice
This makes Jesus the guarantor of a better covenant. The former priests were many in number, because they were prevented by death from continuing in office, but he holds his priesthood permanently, because he continues forever. Consequently, he is able to save to the uttermost those who draw near to God through him, since he always lives to make intercession for them. For it was indeed fitting that we should have such a high priest, holy, innocent, unstained, separated from sinners, and exalted above the heavens. He has no need, like those high priests, to offer sacrifices daily, first for his own sins and then for those of the people, since he did this once for all when he offered up himself.
Heb. 7:22–27

———

As you walk with your friends through their challenges, you will want to keep bringing them to Jesus for them to behold. Praying for Jesus to reveal himself to them and for them to discover how Jesus is the only answer to their questions. It is through a relationship with him that their present and eternal identity crisis can ever be remedied.

Jesus is the Truth. Jesus is God. Jesus is Love. Jesus is God Incarnate. Jesus is Creator. Jesus is the Suffering Servant.

FOLLOW UP
CONVERSATIONS

Always the beautiful answer who asks a more
beautiful question.
—E. E. Cummings, Poems: 1923–1954

*That very day two of them were going to a village named
Emmaus, about seven miles from Jerusalem, and they
were talking with each other about all these things that
had happened. While they were talking and discussing
together, Jesus himself drew near and went with them.
But their eyes were kept from recognizing him. And he
said to them, "What is this conversation that you are
holding with each other as you walk?" And they stood
still, looking sad.*
Luke 24:13–17

Jesus came alongside these two men who were struggling to figure out how to take the next steps in life.

Jesus entered into conversations with them and showed them how everything pointed to him. By grace, he opened their eyes and gave them faith to behold him as the Lord.

We would be wise to do the same with our friends. Alister McGrath explains:

> The apologist is thus presented with the task of making connections between the Christian story and the audience, aiming to show how the gospel has the capacity to help us discover who we are and who we are meant to be to help others see how the Christian story connects with, and eventually transforms, their own personal stories.[1]

One of the best ways I have found to do this is to take my friends on a walk with Jesus in the gospels. They see Jesus loving people with similar challenges, and they can't help but encounter Jesus for themselves. By the Holy Spirit, Jesus begins to speak a more beautiful answer to the questions of their hearts. To prime the pump, I have provided five Follow-Up Conversations for each of the different Identities. The Conversations are gospel passages chosen to help your friends ask more beautiful questions around their identity and the identity of Christ. The Conversations are simple to facilitate and easy to understand.

In each Conversation, you can start by taking turns reading the passage and asking these initial questions:

Do you see the identity challenge or crisis in each of the people mentioned?

What is their posture toward Jesus? Ignorance, Arrogance, or Faith?

What are the questions of their hearts?

What does Jesus say, and how does he respond? What does this tell you about Jesus?

What truths are brought out that we should take to heart?

How can this help you practically in your challenge this week?

At the end of each Follow-up Conversation, close your time by thanking Jesus in prayer and praying for any requests. Also encourage them to read one of the gospels as you are meeting.

After completing the initial Five Follow-up Conversations around their challenged identity, see if they want to go through another identity or look at further verses (from the Old Testament and epistles) in the area they were initially challenged in. Hopefully their hearts will be opened to put their faith in Jesus along the way, begin attending a small group in your church and even begin attending your Sunday gatherings.

May the Lord bless your efforts in sharing the Good News of Jesus Christ!

1. Alister, E. McGrath, *Narrative Apologetics: Sharing the Relevance, Joy, And Wonder of The Christian Faith* (Ada: Baker Books, 2019), 127.

LEARNER FOLLOW-UP CONVERSATIONS

At that time Jesus declared, "I thank you, Father, Lord of heaven and earth, that you have hidden these things from the wise and understanding and revealed them to little children; yes, Father, for such was your gracious will. All things have been handed over to me by my Father, and no one knows the Son except the Father, and no one knows the Father except the Son and anyone

to whom the Son chooses to reveal him. Come to me, all who labor and are heavy laden, and I will give you rest. Take my yoke upon you, and learn from me, for I am gentle and lowly in heart, and you will find rest for your souls. For my yoke is easy, and my burden is light.

Matt. 11:25–30

Conversation #1

Luke 10:38–42 ——— Jesus & Martha, Mary

Conversation #2

John 3:1–21 ——— Jesus & Nicodemus

Conversation #3

John 1:19–34 ——— Jesus & John, Priests, Levites

Conversation #4

Luke 24:13–35 ——— Jesus & Emmaus Road

Conversation #5

John 18:28–19:16 ——— Jesus & Pilate

WORSHIPER FOLLOW-UP
CONVERSATIONS

Worthy are you, our Lord and God, to receive glory and honor and power, for you created all things, and by your will they existed and were created.... Worthy is the Lamb who was slain, to receive power and wealth and wisdom and might and honor and glory and blessing!
Rev. 4:11, 5:12

Conversation #1

Matt. 2:1–12 ———— Jesus & Herod, Magi

Conversation #2

Luke 7:36–50 ———— Jesus & The Sinful Woman

Conversation #3

Mark 9:14–29 ———— Jesus & Desperate Father

Conversation #4

John 20:19–29 ———— Jesus & Disciples, Thomas

Conversation #5

John 4:1–26 ———— Jesus & the Woman of Samaria

BELOVED FOLLOW-UP
CONVERSATIONS

For this reason I bow my knees before the Father, from whom every family in heaven and on earth is named, that according to the riches of his glory he may grant you to be strengthened with power through his Spirit in your inner being, so that Christ may dwell in your hearts through faith—that you, being rooted and grounded in love, may have strength to comprehend with all the

saints what is the breadth and length and height and depth, and to know the love of Christ that surpasses knowledge, that you may be filled with all the fullness of God. Eph. 3:14–19

Conversation #1
John 8:1–11 ——— Jesus & The Adulteress
Conversation #2
Luke 22:54–62, John 21:15–25 ——— Jesus & Peter
Conversation #3
John 11:1–44 ——— Jesus & Lazarus
Conversation #4
Acts 7:54–60 ——— Jesus & Stephen
Conversation #5
John 15:9–17 ——— Jesus & No Greater Love

NEIGHBOR FOLLOW-UP CONVERSATIONS

*Above all, keep loving one another earnestly, since love covers a
multitude of sins. Show hospitality to one another without
grumbling. As each has received a gift, use it to serve one
another, as good stewards of God's varied grace: whoever speaks,
as one who speaks oracles of God; whoever serves, as one who
serves by the strength that God supplies—in order that in every-*

thing God may be glorified through Jesus Christ. To him belong glory and dominion forever and ever. Amen.
1 Pet. 4:8–11

Conversation #1
Matt. 22:34–40 ——— Jesus & Great Commandments
Conversation #2
Luke 10:25–37 ——— Jesus & Good Samaritan
Conversation #3
Luke 23:32–43 ——— Jesus & Two Criminals
Conversation #4
Mark 2:1–12 ——— Jesus & Friends, Paralytic
Conversation #5
Matthew 18:21–35 ——— Jesus & Forgiveness

CULTUREMAKER FOLLOW-UP CONVERSATIONS

I thank my God in all my remembrance of you, always in every prayer of mine for you all making my prayer with joy, because of your partnership in the gospel from the first day until now. And I am sure of this, that he who began a good work in you will bring it to completion at the day of Jesus Christ. It is right for me to feel this way about you all, because I hold you in my heart, for

you are all partakers with me of grace, both in my imprisonment and in the defense and confirmation of the gospel. For God is my witness, how I yearn for you all with the affection of Christ Jesus. And it is my prayer that your love may abound more and more, with knowledge and all discernment, so that you may approve what is excellent, and so be pure and blameless for the day of Christ, filled with the fruit of righteousness that comes through Jesus Christ, to the glory and praise of God.
Phi. 1:3–11

Conversation #1
Matt. 19:16–30 ——— Jesus & Rich Man, Disciples
Conversation #2
Mark 12:13–17 ——— Jesus & Caesar
Conversation #3
Matt. 25:14–30 ——— Jesus & Investing
Conversation #4
Matt. 28:16–20 ——— Jesus & Great Commission
Conversation #5
Acts 9:1–22 ——— Jesus & Saul/Paul

SERVANT FOLLOW-UP
CONVERSATIONS

*Blessed be the God and Father of our Lord Jesus Christ, the
Father of mercies and God of all comfort, who comforts us in all
our affliction, so that we may be able to comfort those who are in
any affliction, with the comfort with which we ourselves are
comforted by God. For as we share abundantly in Christ's sufferings, so through Christ we share abundantly in comfort too. If*

we are afflicted, it is for your comfort and salvation; and if we are comforted, it is for your comfort, which you experience when you patiently endure the same sufferings that we suffer. Our hope for you is unshaken, for we know that as you share in our sufferings, you will also share in our comfort.

2 Cor. 1:3–7

Conversation #1

Matt. 9:18–38 ——— Jesus & Compassion

Conversation #2

John 13:1–20 ——— Jesus Washes the Disciple" Feet

Conversation #3

Matt. 20:20–28 ——— Jesus & a Place of Greatness

Conversation #4

John 10:1–21 ——— Jesus & His Sheep

Conversation #5

Matthew 8:5–17 ——— Jesus & Centurion

MY STORY IN CHRIST'S STORY

I have chosen to end this book with my personal journey in finding my true identity in Christ. As Wendell Berry states, "Telling a story is like reaching into a granary full of wheat and drawing out a handful. There is always more to tell than can be told."[1]

I am sharing my story through personal snapshots that lead up to my marriage—living examples of questions that resided in my heart, even at an early age. I hope it convinces you that no matter what age, circumstance, struggle, or success people are going through, they need a friend to lean in, listen for, and love them well through their identity challenges. At the end of each snapshot, I have included my heart's posture, the identity that was being challenged and a Scripture passage.

I also share my story as a reminder that we should be ready to tell our story with our friends, whether a shorter or in a longer version. This can help illustrate our own desperate need for the Gospel. Personal stories can bring about a curiosity, prompting the listener to ponder the meaning of their own story. Charlie Peacock writes, "Knowing the story you are participating in will affect the person you become."[2] The Lord places us in people's lives for many reasons. Sometimes, if not most of the time, our story is that very reason.

Ed Welch explains the value of sharing our stories:

> It doesn't get much better than hearing someone's story. Knowing and being known. Openness. A growing friendship. And as we grow in these things, we should expect this general rule: the better you know other people, the more you enjoy and appreciate them—that is, the more you love them. And the more you love them, the more you will be invited into their lives during hardships"[3]

I have called these hardships challenges and crises.

As you go through and begin to have questions of the heart conversations, I encourage you to sit down and type out your journey with God and how your identity has been challenged along the way. It will humble you and remind you of how God has never left you, and how he has changed your identity—one degree of glory to the next.

Why Can't I Just Be Like Everyone Else—Normal?!

The struggle for my identity began even before I could crawl. I was born with Spina Bifida, and I was labeled "defective" from the get-go. They said I may never walk, but after several surgeries the Lord had different plans.

The doctors used my big sister to coax me to stand up and stumble across the room. I thought it was cruel, but the doctors called them miracle steps. If being thought of as defective wasn't tough enough, try being called a miracle. Words have a powerful effect on our psyche, and they shape our identity.

These first physical steps were not my miraculous ones. I spent the first twenty years of my life chasing after approval and pleasure rather than trusting God for my identity. Early on, the question deep within my heart was, "Why can't I just be like everyone else—normal?!"

I didn't take any chances, so I hid my disabilities. Our culture applauds the strong and has very little to say about the weak. You can imagine my surprise when I found out later in Scripture that God prefers to use the weak things in the world to reveal his glory.

Posture: Ignorance
Challenged Identity: Orphan, Loner

But he said to me, "My grace is sufficient for you, for my power is made perfect in weakness." Therefore, I will

> *boast all the more gladly of my weaknesses, so that the*
> *power of Christ may rest upon me.*
> 2 Cor. 12:9

How Can I Get More Applause?!

I had a strange notion that God owed me a good life because he had initially dealt me such a bad hand. This entitlement mentality fueled my risk-taking, and it led to a subtle arrogance that I could get away with almost anything. My parents curbed this restlessness by throwing me into a pool all year round.

I became Aquaman. I was pumped when they recently brought back the web-handed wonder to the movies. He's a bit more fit and tatted this time around, but I've always been a fan.

In contrast, I was like those little black water bugs—small but fast. Our summer swim team modified the television theme song from "Flipper," to "Thumper, Thumper faster than lightning" to spur my two sisters and I on to victory. "Thumper" was my nickname, and it has stuck with me.

Summers at Colonial Country Club were some of my fondest memories, because in the pool I was like all the other kids—but faster. I experienced success early on in my speedo, so the question of my heart was more bragging than inquiry: "How can I get more applause?! How could this team make it without me? MVP baby!" It's amazing what a few blue ribbons and gold medals can do to a prideful heart.

Posture: Arrogance
Challenged Identity: Entitled, Narcissist

Pride goes before destruction, and a haughty spirit before
a fall.
Prov. 16:18

Do I Have What It Takes?!

When I turned ten years old, we moved from Missis-
sippi to South Carolina, a huge leap in the state educa-
tional ranking—last to second-to-last. I kept swimming
through middle school and on into high school at a
much higher level for the Paladins Aquatic Club at
Furman University.

Before the crack of dawn, my dad would take me to
practice. After school, I would catch a ride back for a
few more miles between the lane ropes. The competi-
tion got more intense, and this little black waterbug
standing at 4' 11" didn't have a chance against the 6'
leviathans. As I caught my breath between butterfly
strokes, the question sloshing around in my heart was,
"Do I have what it takes?!" John Eldridge, the author of
You Have What It Takes, writes, "Every boy wants to be a
hero. Every boy wants to be powerful; he wants to be
dangerous, and he wants to know: Do I have what it
takes? And every boy looks to his dad to answer it."[4]

Posture: Ignorance, Arrogance
Challenged Identity: Orphan, Whiner

*And when Jesus was baptized, immediately he went up
from the water, and behold, the heavens were opened to
him, and he saw the Spirit of God descending like a dove
and coming to rest on him; and behold, a voice from
heaven said, "This is my beloved Son, with whom I am
well pleased.*

Matt. 3:16–17

I Guess I'm on My Own?!

My dad was a lean, handsome man. In his younger days,
he was a chubby lad with black curly locks. He found his
place on the greens and was offered to play golf for
several colleges, but he didn't go due for reasons of
his own.

He went off to the Army and a few years of junior
college. I wonder if he regretted that decision, but don't
we all wish we could have a couple mulligans in life? He
was a natural salesman and won many awards. Gradu-
ally, he made his way back to the family trade. He
opened up his own typography studio near an old pipe
store. I remember going to work with him and he'd stop
off for a few puffs of Kentucky Select Blend and a cup of
coffee. I'd get a cup also, one part coffee, three parts
water, and one too many sugar cubes.

He was a quiet man, a smoker, creative yet desul-
tory. He inherited a flair for cars and would often come
home with a new ride from work. This frustrated mom
to no end, but I thought it was pretty cool. That
wasn't the only thing that got in between them, and
things got real confusing on the homefront. Our home

had many walls, but not the kind you hang a picture on.

I knew something was wrong even from the age of twelve. I remember going into my parents' room and asking them point blank, "Dad! Tell mom you love her! Mom! Tell dad you love him!" There was silence. I walked out that day with the question pounding in my heart: "I guess I'm on my own?!"

I envied my friends' families and spent most of my time at their homes rather than mine. We would have sleepovers, play kick-the-can at the twins' house, and run all over Devenger subdivision playing hide-and-seek. In the summer months, I set up residence at the community pool. It had showers and vending machines to cover all the necessities. Just as summer ended, so did my parent's marriage. My earlier prediction had nurtured in me a strong independent spirit that stiffens my neck even to this day. Much later, I would discover that Jesus would never leave me nor forsake me, and that he was preparing a place just for me in his home.

Posture: Ignorance
Challenged Identity: Loner

And behold, I am with you always, to the end of the age.
Matt. 28:20

How Can I Get the Girls?!

As I moved into my early teen years, I became a jack-of-all-identities. I let my surroundings determine who I was. I fit in almost anywhere, a shapeshifter of sorts. I went from one friend group to the next. I never let anyone ever get too close. From the outside, you would think I was confident and secure in my identity, but I had no moorings whatsoever.

My preoccupation of making waves in the pool quickly turned to my fascination with trying to do the same with the ladies. At that age, it was more about the chase than the catch. My school didn't lack for cute girls, so I spent most of my time trying to get their attention.

Since they were all taller than me, I had to work extra hard to measure up. At one dance, I had to stand on a step stool to slow dance with a 5' 8" hottie— smooth, real smooth. I'll have to show you one of my patchwork sport coat pics sometime.

The challenge and question of my heart was, "How can I get the girls?!" We were all little politicians campaigning and using our friendships to prop up our fledgling egos. What seemed so harmless back then would begin my addiction for the approval of others. In *Counterfeit Gods*, Tim Keller writes:

An idol is whatever you look at and say, in your heart of hearts, "If I have that, then I'll feel my life has meaning, then I'll know I have value, then I'll feel significant and secure." There are many ways to describe that kind of relationship to something, but perhaps the best one is worship.[5]

Posture: Ignorance, Arrogance
Challenged Identity: Idolator, Politician

Every man is stupid and without knowledge; every gold-
smith is put to shame by his idols, for his images are
false, and there is no breath in them. They are worthless,
a work of delusion....
Jer. 51:17–18a

If She Really Knew Me, Would She Accept Me?!

I turned to my middle sister, Sherry, for help in the girl department. She insisted on a new wardrobe and threw out my favorite brown, tough-skin jeans with knee patches and my two-sizes-too-big Keebler Elf shirt. It was a travesty, but the ladies were worth the sacrifice.

Sherry was the white sheep of the family. Everything she touched turned to gold. She was a tremendous swimmer and runner, having to compete with the guys on the track to keep things interesting. She was beautiful, fourth in the Face of the '80s modeling contest. I tried to follow in her footsteps competing in Mr. Riverside. I finished as a finalist, but was beat out by a guy named Gurley who looked like Rob Lowe.

St. Elmo's Fire was a hit that year, so none of us had a chance. My friendship with Gurley worked out to my advantage though. I was his wing man on a few occasions. Sherry was a cheerleader along with five other girls with names beginning with "S." I went out with one of her friends, but it didn't go so well. On the date, she asked me how much I thought she weighed, and I overshot by thirty pounds. Lesson learned!

Later in high school, it became more about the relationship than the chase. Hormones are the jolt of lightning that turn teenagers into monsters. My boss rented a hotel suite for all my friends for an after-dance party. A stupid move on his part.

I left to pick up some snacks and came back—the door was kicked down, the jacuzzi was smashed, coolers were dumped out pouring water into the room below, and red PJ was splattered on the punched-in walls like a crime scene. I went home and never reported back to work. In the midst of all the insanity, I had a few relationships that lasted for a while, but the fear of letting someone truly in sealed off my heart. The question plagued me: "If she really knew me, would she accept me?!" I was too afraid and selfish to trust or to be trusted, so I settled for running away from one shallow, momentary escapade to the next.

Posture: Ignorance
Challenged Identity: Orphan, Loner

Where shall I go from your Spirit? Or where shall I flee from your presence? If I ascend to heaven, you are there! If I make my bed in Sheol, you are there! If I take the wings of the morning and dwell in the uttermost parts of the sea, even there your hand shall lead me, and your right hand shall hold me. If I say, "Surely the darkness shall cover me, and the light about me be night," even the

*darkness is not dark to you; the night is bright as the
day, for darkness is as light with you."*
Ps. 139:7–12

God Why Are You So Against Her?!

My oldest sister, Kristie, was a master at partying, and
she took me under her wing. Big Kickie, my term of
endearment for her, was expelled from kindergarten for
biting everyone. She was nicknamed "Jaws" thereafter.
Along with biting, she was a music lover—Duran
Duran, Bon Jovi, The Dead Milkmen, Bob Geldof,
Culture Club, and The Doors were her favorites, along
with Melissa Etheridge and Madonna.

She was the black sheep of the family and stood toe
to toe with mom. Kristie was the first female member of
the "Labelists," a high school drinking club that prided
themselves on the finest of stouts, *Black Label*.

She snuck out for late night concerts more than she
slept in her own bed. She could make straight As but
rarely showed up for class. She would dip a whole can of
Copenhagen in one night, wear plaid wool pants and
add-a-beads with attitude, drink a case of beer on more
than one occasion, and knew every song of the eighties.
What a woman!

She didn't finish high school, instead settling for a
GED. Kristie went on to study at the Music Business
Institute in Atlanta, where she made music videos
before MTV and did her share of drugs. She was asked
to go on the road with Stevie Ray Vaughn, but she was
too messed up to pull it off.

One night in high school, I found the apartment door wide open and the bathroom splattered with her blood. I frantically searched every hospital until I found her rocking in the fetal position in the ER. I often cried out to God on her behalf: *"God why are you so against her?!"* She didn't fit into this world, but later it wouldn't matter because God had designed her for another one. She tried church on several occasions, but they never gave her a backstage pass.

Posture: Arrogance
Challenged Identity: Cynic

Jesus stood up and said to her, "Woman, where are they? Has no one condemned you?" She said, "No one, Lord." And Jesus said, "Neither do I condemn you; go, and from now on sin no more.
John 8:10–11

How Can I Appear Good and Still Enjoy Doing What's Wrong?!

I wanted to be like both of my two amazing sisters. I wanted a little bit of Sherry, the white sheep, getting the perks of doing things right, and some of Kristie, the black sheep, living for the party. I settled on somewhere in between as the grey sheep of the family. I was trying to answer the question, "How can I appear good and still enjoy doing what's wrong?!" When people were watching, I played the innocent lamb; and when they turned their heads, I howled at the moon. I look back now and marvel that all three of us needed Jesus—Sherry trusting in her own good deeds, Kristie shaking her fist at God, and me in my duplicity. We all wandered in our own way, but the Good Shepherd left the ninety-seven and came after us three.

Posture: Ignorance
Challenged Identity: Fool

Woe to you, scribes and Pharisees, hypocrites! For you are like whitewashed tombs, which outwardly appear beautiful, but within are full of dead people's bones and all uncleanness. So you also outwardly appear righteous to others, but within you are full of hypocrisy and lawlessness.
Matt. 23:27–28

How Can She Love Me So Much Even though I Continue to Break Her Heart?!

My mom stepped in and rescued me when the divorce was final. I'd been evicted from the apartment where my dad and I lived. I had thrown a Pee-wee Herman party. We watched the movie, and you had to drink every time Pee-wee laughed—*"huh, huh, huh, haaaah, huh, huh."* The owners left a note early in the morning after everyone had left. It was for my dad, and it said, "You can stay, but your son has got to GO!!!!"

Thankfully in divorce court, my mom asked for nothing else but me.

My mom was the oldest of five children from the

dirt-paved little town of Gray Court, South Carolina. She was Miss Laurens County. Her legs won her that honor, along with her green eyes and brunette beehive. Those legs of hers not only won awards, but also took her off the family's forty-acre farm to Anderson College. She was the first to go to college. She settled into a political life of sorts working for the Equal Employment Opportunity Commission, investigating job discrimination cases, and in her spare time campaigned for various causes.

She was sophisticated, a Gloria Steinem-type feminist, and she wanted the world to know a woman could hold her own. Her career ended prematurely due to a recurring brain tumor. This still didn't stop her from caring for me. Her depth of love and kindness would point me down the road to a greater love that Jesus demonstrated on the cross. In the Bible, Romans says it is the riches of God's kindness, forbearance, and patience that leads us to repentance.

I moved in with my mom and transferred to a different high school. I shaved off my cheesy mustache and rat tail, put on a Ralph Lauren polo, and created a fresh new identity at Eastside High School. Around this time, my mother's brain tumor came back, and she had another surgery. I wasn't much help this time, and I had the gall to lie about her illness to get off work to go party.

When she found out, it broke her heart. It was one of the first times I saw her pain and disappointment in me. My guilt and shame pricked my conscience. I realized I wasn't as good as I thought I was. I often wondered, "Why do I keep treating her this way? I'm not that wicked am I? How can she love me so much even though I continue to break her heart?!"

You might be thinking at this point, "Duh, it's pretty obvious you were a punk! If it looks like a duck and quacks like a duck, then it's probably a duck."

But I wasn't much different from most of the others I ran with, no offense to them. We all thought we were good kids all in all. We just had a skewed measuring stick—doing what was right in our own eyes. I knew I was doing wrong, but I just couldn't stop, or I didn't want to stop.

Posture: Arrogance
Challenged Identity: Entitled, Narcissist

For I do not understand my own actions. For I do not do what I want, but I do the very thing I hate.
Ro. 7:15

God If You Can Hear Me, Help?!

At seventeen, my identity was wrapped up in my black T-top Datsun 260z, chasing girls and twelve-packs. Ironically, I had a fake ID business helping others create false identities along with me. Most of my drinking buddies and I got DUIs and almost flunked out of school. I got mine speeding to the College of Charleston listening to the Beastie Boys: "Four and three and two and one. What up!" [6]

Then blue lights, sirens, and a night in the slammer.

My friend and I stammered into the Orangeburg Minimum Security filled with guys screaming, "I need some crack! I need some crack! The dogs are gonna be barking tonight!" Dressed in tight green jumpsuits, the question in my heart at that moment was, "Are they screaming at us for drugs or something else? God if you can hear me, Help?!"

We took turns watching each other's back—playing cards with the Godfather of the jail, whose tongue had been cut out. We also learned how to disassemble a pistol in under a minute with the help of the gun magazines.

Sitting in a jail cell makes you think about freedom. Most people live in prisons they create for themselves. Even though they could be free, they choose to live locked up in fear, sorrow, anger and pride.

Posture: Ignorance
Challenged Identity: Idolater, Orphan

Jesus answered them, "Truly, truly, I say to you, everyone who practices sin is a slave to sin…. So if the Son sets you free, you will be free indeed."
John 8:34, 36

How Am I Going to Get Myself Out of This One?!

My buddy and I didn't hurt anyone, so it didn't have the impact you might think it would. It gave us a great story to tell everyone. I hadn't learned my lesson, and I got busted soon after for buying beer with the Captain of

Police's son. The question of my heart in the back of the police car was, "How am I going to get myself out of this one?!"

You know that saying, "It's not what you know, but who you know that matters." Let's just say I used that to my advantage, though I did lose my license. Not to sound irreverent, but I was going to find out later that I would need to know someone else to get me off much greater charges—eternal ones in fact.

Posture: Ignorance
Challenged Identity: Fool, Orphan

And this is eternal life, that they know you, the only true God, and Jesus Christ whom you have sent.
John 17:3

Trying This Won't Hurt Me?!

I tried to slow down a bit, especially because I couldn't drive anymore, but working in a restaurant with pockets full of tips and no curfew didn't help. While we were spinning trays and slinging food, my friends and I at the Steak House had way too much fun. I have toyed with the idea of writing a book about the culture of late-night restaurants: *Waiting for Life.* Everyone is just buying time until they get their big break. Sadly, many never get out and end up perpetually waiting for life.

I didn't have big aspirations or even think much about the future. I was content with just living for the moment. Hanging out with an older crowd in restaurants is dangerous for a young guy. It creates a longing to experience now what you never should at your age or any age for that matter. Like an addict, your cravings are never satisfied. You're always wanting more. I wasn't asking as much as I was stating: "Trying this won't hurt me?!" Even though I was surrounded with prime rib and filet mignon, everything in my life was tasteless. I experimented with drugs and began going further into darkness.

Posture: Ignorance
Challenged Identity: Consumer

Vanity of vanities, says the Preacher; all is vanity.
Ecc. 12:8

Could There Be Something More to Life than This?!

By the end of high school, my heart was covered with scars from sins and wounds. I was a cheater, a liar, a drunk and an all-around nice guy. The poet Joyce Rachelle writes: "Some scars don't hurt. Some scars are numb. Some scars rid you of the capacity to feel anything ever again."[7] Despite intense numbness, my heart would still thud from time to time, "Could there be something more to life than this?!"

This question prompted me to escape to college. I didn't know what I was looking for, but college seemed like a great place to buy time with my friends as I figured it out.

Posture: Ignorance, Arrogance
Challenged Identity: Fool, Whiner

My son, if you receive my words and treasure up my commandments with you, making your ear attentive to wisdom and inclining your heart to understanding; yes, if you call out for insight and raise your voice for understanding, if you seek it like silver and search for it as for hidden treasures, then you will understand the fear of the LORD and find the knowledge of God.
Prov. 2:1–5

Maybe I Can Find Myself in College?!

My best friend and I went off to a small college in Banner Elk, North Carolina, thanks to its low GPA requirements. I thought I could discover myself snow skiing and reclining next to a roaring fire in the Beech and Sugar Mountain lodges. I wondered: "Maybe I can find myself in college?!" It was a Presbyterian college, but I still preferred queuing up at the keg than the line for communion. Growing up, my mom had taken our family to First Presbyterian Church in Greenville. She had high hopes that I would attend a religious school. While I wasn't antagonistic toward church, I didn't have a need for it. I had read parts of the Bible, but I had never let the Bible read me.

You've heard the saying, "There's bears in dem dar hills." Well, it got a bit hairy up there—dreadlocked earthies walking around in the snow with no shoes, dorm fights, gun-totin' old timers on the river, twenty-

five cent draft on Thursday nights, and Harley David-
sons dragging coffins down the Blue Ridge Viaducts.
There was one night when the women's dorm at the
top of the hill picked a fight with the one at the bottom
of the hill. It was a vicious brawl between a hundred
young coeds, a melee of braids and ponytails. All the
guys sat on the grassy knoll in disbelief muttering,
"You goin' down there to break it up? Are *you*?" The
whole police department had to come out and lock it
down. Even though we loved skiing, my best friend and
I had had enough. After a year, we headed back down
South.

Posture: Arrogance
Challenged Identity: Cynic

*I said in my heart, "Come now, I will test you with plea-
sure; enjoy yourself." But behold, this also was vanity."*
Ecc. 2:1

Why God? Why Did You Allow This to Happen? Don't You Care?!

One moment stands out on that frozen mountain. A
student from our hometown and I got a call about my
best friend's mother. She had unexpectedly passed away.
We had to tell him.

It was one of the hardest things I have ever had to
do. It brings tears to my eyes even now as I type this. I
had lost people before, but I never had to be the bearer
of news so weighty, so personal, so life changing.

Holding him in his pain, rage and sorrow awakened in me the reality of life and death.

My heart cried out in pain: "Why God? Why did you allow this to happen? Don't you care?!" Little did I know that God would be calling me two years later to be the bearer of the weightiest news in the world—the message of Jesus Christ's death. Suffering and pain are not in the world because God doesn't care or is vindictive. It's the very reason he sent his Son into the world. He came to suffer in our place and to make our suffering part of glory. Seasons of suffering are some of the most vulnerable moments in our lives, when our hearts are asking profound questions—a time when a true friend can make all the difference in their world.

Posture: Ignorance
Challenged Identity: Orphan

"O death, where is your victory? O death, where is your sting?" But thanks be to God, who gives us the victory through our Lord Jesus Christ.
1 Cor. 15:55–57

What Is My Purpose in Life?!

The University of South Carolina was my next stop, and SAE became my fraternity. There is something to say about being a part of a fraternity: the camaraderie of your pledge class, a big brother looking out for you, and a tribe in the midst of thirty-thousand savages. The letters SAE defined me for the next two years with a secret handshake, chillin in the lounge, parties with sororities, football tailgates, and some of the greatest guys in the world.

Oh, I almost forgot—getting a degree. It was here that the question of my heart turned to: "What is my purpose in life?!" If you would have told anybody that I was going to become a pastor, they would have thought you were mad, but our God has a great sense of humor.

Posture: Ignorance
Challenged Identity: Consumer, Fool

Q. 1. What is the chief end of man?
A. 1. Man's chief end is to glorify God, and to enjoy him forever.
—Westminster Shorter Catechism

What Helped Him Overcome?!

My dorm was the infamous Honeycombs which were torn down soon after I graduated. But who can complain with tuition only being $5000. I'm hesitant to say, "You get what you pay for" with all my Clemson friends listening.

I roomed with a jolly old soul who was majoring in journalism. He would get a kick out of me writing a book knowing that I only read one book all the way through high school. He wasn't labeled "defective" but rather "disabled." He was one of the strongest people I knew despite being confined to a wheelchair.

His story is a tragic one. His father was flying the

family on a trip in their private plane when conditions turned for the worse. The plane crashed and killed everyone on board except my roommate. He survived, but his injuries left him paralyzed from the waist down. Often, I wondered: "How in the world did he cope with such loss and devastation? What helped him overcome?!" In my shallowness, I never broached the subject, but my entitlement took a hit from his unexplained joy.

Posture: Arrogance
Challenged Identity: Entitlement

The Lord is near to the brokenhearted and saves the
crushed in spirit.
Ps. 34:18

Do You Have a Personal Relationship with Jesus Christ?!

I got a job waiting tables at Columbia's, a four-star restaurant on the corner of Gervais and Assembly. I made over $100 in tips on good nights. Regretfully, I promptly spent it in Five Points at the Elbow Room and Green Streets, where Hootie and the Blowfish got their start.

There was also an older SAE fraternity brother that worked at Columbia's. He had become a Christian earlier that year. You would never guess that he had been addicted to cocaine. He saw a lot in me that used to be in him, so he leaned in, listened for the questions of my heart, and loved me well. He became a good friend, and I began asking the deeper questions of the heart. One day, he pulled me aside and asked if I was a Christian. Even though he knew I wasn't, he wanted me to answer it for myself.

I responded, "Sure I went to church when I was younger and go to church sometimes on Christmas and Easter. I know I'm doing some things that I shouldn't right now, but deep down I'm a pretty good guy."

He received that answer with grace and then asked me another: "Do you have a personal relationship with Jesus Christ?!"

I didn't quite know how to answer. I said, "Uhhh.... Well, I've never been asked that before." He later asked if I would be willing to go to a bible study with a few other guys.

I didn't think much of it, so I said, "Why not?"

Posture: Ignorance
Challenged Identity: Fool

Walk in wisdom toward outsiders, making the best use of the time. Let your speech always be gracious, seasoned with salt, so that you may know how you ought to answer each person.
Col. 4:5–6

Jesus Isn't Really Who I Thought He Was?!

The bible study I had agreed to attend was a group of four guys that met each week to talk about what mattered most in their lives, consider a few Bible passages, and pray for each other. Up to that point, I had thought most Christians were a bunch of socially inept goodie two-shoes, so I was surprised that these dudes were pretty cool, as if I was a good judge of coolness.

I began attending off and on, but I still blew it out with my frat brothers the rest of the time. One night after a big keg party, I started sharing what I had learned in our Bible study with a couple of my fraternity brothers. I'm not sure what my first sermon sounded like, but they had fun laughing about it nonetheless. I had many mixed thoughts and emotions tumbling in my heart, but I was actually starting to listen.

Studying the Bible made me ask, "Could this be true?! I thought I knew God and what was in the Bible. Jesus isn't really who I thought he was?!" Just like everybody else, I had my opinion about who Jesus was. Some are willing to claim he was a good, moral teacher, but he healed the lame, forgave sin, and walked on water. His claims and actions don't allow for the option that was merely a good, moral teacher. As C. S. Lewis concluded, Jesus is either a liar, Lord, or lunatic.

Posture: Faith
Identity: Learner

And he asked them, "Who do the crowds say that I am?"
And they answered, "John the Baptist. But others say,
Elijah, and others, that one of the prophets of old has

risen." Then he said to them, "But who do you say that I
am?" And Peter answered, "The Christ of God."
Luke 9:18–20

Kevin, Is This What You Want for Your Life?!

As I teetered on the fence of faith, God began pressing
in on my heart. I'll never forget one night around two
o'clock at Group Therapy, an end-of-the-road dive bar, I
sat dazed looking around at the drunken motley crew.
All of a sudden, I was stone-cold sober. As I looked
around again, God began to speak to my heart, "Kevin,
is this what you want for your life?! I have so much
more for you. Come follow me." It wasn't an audible
voice or anything, but a deep echo in my soul of the
Scriptures we had been studying. In Hebrews 4:12–13,
we read:

> *For the word of God is living and active, sharper than*
> *any two-edged sword, piercing to the division of soul and*
> *of spirit, of joints and of marrow, and discerning the*
> *thoughts and intentions of the heart. And no creature is*
> *hidden from his sight, but all are naked and exposed to*
> *the eyes of him to whom we must give account.*

That night the Word of God did surgery on my soul,
cutting out my heart of stone and giving me a heart of
flesh. It took weeks of wrestling for my head and confes-
sion to catch up with my heart. Like Jacob, I wrestled
not letting go, and God let me win.

That is the beauty of the Gospel, God lets sinners

win! On February 28, 1990, I got on my knees and cried out to God in repentance of my sin and rebellion toward him.

So many of the questions of my heart flooded through my mind as I prayed and wept. As I took a good look at myself, I understood for the first time that I wasn't a good guy no matter what standard I had measured myself with previously. The Bible study had shown me that God was holy and required perfect righteousness. Because my sin and rebellion was a personal affront to God and not just against other people, I was his enemy justly deserving his wrath.

There was nothing I could do to remedy this—no good deed, no religious practice nor promise to earn it with clean living. I also understood that God offered his own remedy by sending his Son Jesus to live a perfect life for me and to exchange his righteousness for my unrighteousness. He took the penalty I deserved by dying on the cross and gave me what only he deserves— eternal life, joy, honor, and glory.

My whole life I had exchanged the truth of God for a lie and worshiped the creature rather than my Creator. In his kindness, the questions of my heart turned to repentance—I turned from my sin and pride into the arms of Jesus. I wasn't just trusting Jesus to make me a better person. I bowed my heart to him by faith as my Lord and Savior.

Jesus became the answer to all the questions of my heart and the Yes to all the promises of God. On that day I found my true identity and took my miracle steps in Christ! My new identity was challenged almost daily, but I was his now, and he was mine. I grew to understand that Jesus invited me to bring all the questions of my heart to him every step of the way.

Posture: Faith
Identity: Worshiper, Culturemaker

Let us then with confidence draw near to the throne of grace, that we may receive mercy and find grace to help in time of need.
Heb. 4:16

Wow God! Wow?!

Everything was different—a good kind of different, a brand new type of different with new eyes, a new heart, and a new purpose. I was alive like I had never been before. C. S. Lewis captures it well when he writes, "I believe in Christianity as I believe that the Sun has risen not only because I see it but because by it I see everything else."[8]

My purpose in college quickly changed from trying to be the life of the party to taking LIFE to the party. People were no longer white noise in the background but present and peculiar. The woman in the business suit, the skateboarder consumed in his music, the homeless man curled up in the nook, and the man walking his dog were all important now.

I was seeing with the eyes of Christ for the first time. It was like putting on EnChroma glasses for the color-blind. My previously gray existence became filled with color. My heart was shouting, "Wow God! Wow?!"

My fraternity brothers thought I had taken a pill that would wear off, but it was more like choosing the Red Pill, where *The Matrix* scales fell off my eyes, from whence there was no return. I had been born again.

Posture: Faith
Identity: Learner

Jesus answered him [Nicodemus], "Truly, truly, I say to you, unless one is born again he cannot see the kingdom of God."
John 3:3

Are You More Excited about the New and Improved Kevin or about Jesus?!

I had to tell everyone! I wanted everyone to experience what I had. I was rather obnoxious about it early on, and I told every person who gave me the time of day. I was like the UPS commercials that go on and on about what they do along with shipping. "Jesus did this, and this, and he does that, and you wouldn't believe what he did yesterday and this morning."

If I wasn't telling someone about Jesus, I was learning more about him. I devoured the Bible, went to college ministries, attended church, and prayed as I went from one thing to the next. I was a sponge and couldn't get enough.

While my non-Christian friends didn't quite know

what to do with me, my new Christian friends did. They gave me opportunities to share my story. There weren't many frat guys excited about Jesus, so I was placed in the spotlight and handed the mic.

After a while, my newfound identity in Christ was challenged with all the attention I was getting. It was subtle, but I had exchanged my pursuit of approval in the party scene to the Christian scene. I'll never forget the rush I felt the first time sharing my story at the USC FCA Night. The place was packed, and all eyes were on me. The applause was more intoxicating than a pint of Jack Daniels. People were much more impressed with the Christian version of Kevin than my previous "me." I was too—that was the problem! It took a while, but my heart began to convict me with the question: "Are you more excited about the new and improved Kevin or about Jesus?!"

One day after I had spent a couple hours spiritually one-upping everyone, a girl who I thought was quite snobbish came out and said it, "Every time you open your mouth, I just want to vomit. You are sooo arrogant. Kevin's doing this, and Kevin's doing that. It makes me sick."

In false humility, I said, "Thanks for being honest. I know I've been struggling with pride."

She said, "Ugghhh... That!... Your answer... That's what I mean! You are so full of yourself."

Faithful are the wounds of a friend; profuse are the kisses of an enemy. Prov. 27:6

I wouldn't have called her my friend at that moment, but she sure made a wound—a much-needed wound. When our identity is radically challenged, a sense of pride can quickly follow. Some have coined it as being "holier-than-thou." My friend preferred, "Kevin you are full of yourself"

We convey that we have figured it all out, and we belittle people in our spiritual hubris. We position others in our shadow rather than lifting them up to bask in the light of Christ. We convey "been there and done that" rather than bending down to wash their feet as Jesus did. Our enthusiasm to fix people silences the cries of their pain and vulnerability. It would do our egos well to ponder early on that the only self-description Jesus made of himself was, *"I am gentle and lowly of heart"* (Matt. 11:29).

The disciples struggled with pride soon after they began to follow Jesus.

Posture: Arrogance
Challenged Identity: Expert, Politician, Narcissist

And they came to Capernaum. And when he was in the house he asked them, "What were you discussing on the way?" But they kept silent, for on the way they had argued with one another about who was the greatest. And he sat down and called the twelve. And he said to them, "If anyone would be first, he must be last of all and servant of all."
Mark 9:33–35

How Can I Get Out of College the Fastest and Not Be Able to Get a Job?!

Our craving for glory isn't wrong in and of itself, for we were designed for glory. However Romans tells us our problem comes when we exchange the glory of God for images, and we worship the created rather than our Creator. We are no different today, except that our preferred image is our own image. The generosity of the Gospel is that Jesus delights in sharing his glory with us.

Instead of us chasing after a name for ourselves like they did at the tower of Babel in Genesis 11, Jesus places his name and glory upon us and transforms us from one degree of glory to the next.

> And we all, with unveiled face, beholding the glory of the
> Lord, are being transformed into the same image from
> one degree of glory to another. For this comes from the
> Lord who is the Spirit.
> 2 Cor. 3:18

Since my faith didn't wear off, my fraternity made me the chaplain and head of philanthropy.

One of the guys in my original Bible study was also in a fraternity, so we began praying over the fraternity quad. We asked God to raise up a handful of fraternity brothers and sorority sisters to come to know Jesus. One by one they came: a Pi Kappa Alpha, an Alpha Tau Omega, a Kappa Delta, and an Alpha Delta Pi.

Together, we organized dry mixers where we shared

our testimonies. Even Governor David Beasley came and shared his faith journey at one of the events. There was a running joke on the fraternity hall about who got stuck with Kevin today. I did have some great conversations with the guys, but not much was remembered the next morning. I regret that I tried to force the issue on them and didn't lean in, listen for, and love them well.

A few months in, I realized I needed to be mentored so I looked for one. The Lord sent me Adrian Depres. He had been a football player at Furman University and was nuts about Jesus.

He helped me and several other young men. Adrian leaned into our lives and loved us well. He taught us, prayed with us, answered our questions, and took us on speaking engagements to share the Gospel with thousands of athletes and college students.

At first I thought he wasn't afraid to share the Gospel with anyone because he was so big, but after a while I understood that he feared God more than man. He wasn't big. God was!

The Lord also gave me a band of brothers—Johnny G, Ben Breazeale, and Chris Murphy. They shaped my faith more than any other men in my life. We grew up in our faith together and partnered in basketball ministry with low income kids, worked in the park with the homeless, and challenged each other to be faithful in our relationships, work, and education.

I was a business major at the time. Before Christ, I wanted to make as much money as possible. Sitting in a finance class that semester, I thought, "Get me outta here! I want the riches of the Kingdom not the riches of this world anymore!"

To my chagrin, I went to my advisor that day and asked her, "How can I get out of college the fastest and *not* be able to get a job?!"

My thinking wasn't clear at the time. I hadn't learned about the priesthood of all believers, where there is no secular and sacred divide in our work, so I thought ministry was the only valid option for me. I didn't want to live a second-rate Christian life. If I could get a good paying job, then I might back out of going into the ministry. So I wanted *to not* get a job.

She looked at me with concern and then perused my transcript and said, "Well, that's easy. Psychology." So I became a psych major with a minor in business, and I planned to graduate in fifteen months.

Posture: Ignorance
Challenged Identity: Fool

And whatever you do, in word or deed, do everything in the name of the Lord Jesus, giving thanks to God the Father through him.
Col. 3:17

God Show Me You Can Change a Guy Like Him?!

Later that semester, I got more involved with Campus Crusade (CRU). They challenged me to go on a summer mission trip, so Johnny G and I headed to Panama City Beach, Florida with students from various colleges around the United States. It was quite the adventure. We studied the book of Colossians and learned to share our faith all over the beach. On Saturdays, we would dress up and play slo-mo football to gather a crowd and then break up and tell them, "We are a bunch of college students that love to have fun, and we love Jesus. If you stick around, we would love to tell you more about him." Part of me wondered if these people took us seriously since we looked crazy in our costumes, but it did attract a crowd and created opportunities to share the Gospel.

The staff left halfway through the summer and gave the students different roles of leadership. I was put in charge of evangelistic outreaches. The evangelism outreach team put together individual evangelistic challenges, small group outings, and outreaches that included everyone. It was amazing how many opportunities open up when you make sharing the Gospel one of your highest priorities.

One night, I went next door to a hotel where tons of bikers camped out. A few of us sat down and began having conversations.

One man and his young daughter caught my eye. His name was Aaron. As our conversation moved along, I was compelled to listen to the questions of his heart rather than give an evangelistic pitch. He opened up, saying that he knew he shouldn't be there with his daughter.

I told him that I would help them with bus fare to get back home. But I challenged him that changing the pond wouldn't change the duck. The real change needed to take place in his heart. I shared the Gospel, prayed for them, "God give Aaron and his daughter a new life. Show him that you are real," and I left.

The question in my heart was, "God show me you can change a guy like him?!" The next morning, he was sitting in our hotel lobby shaking and ready to go home. I bought him a ticket and off they went. A month later back at USC, I got a hand-written letter from Aaron. He told me that he hadn't been fully honest with me.

He wasn't just running from his past but from the law. There was a warrant out for his arrest for grand theft auto. He said that he had taken a long hard look at himself in the mirror that night and given his life to Jesus. He had gone home and left his daughter with his mom and turned himself in. He was now serving five years in prison, but he was more free than he had ever been in his life. He had plenty of time to read the Bible and to share the Gospel with the other inmates. He was let out on good behavior a year and a half later.

Posture: Faith
Identity: Neighbor, Servant

Jesus answered them, "Truly, truly, I say to you, everyone who practices sin is a slave to sin. The slave does not remain in the house forever; the son remains forever. So if the Son sets you free, you will be free indeed."
John 8:34–36

Trust Me?!

The most significant thing I faced on the summer mission trip was telling my roommates about my ongoing challenges of Spina Bifida. These guys listened, heard my heart, and loved me well. At that point, I had never told anyone.

I had gone to my doctor earlier in the year, and he told me about a surgery which I could undergo to hopefully take care of the issues. I prayed about it, and I heard deep in my heart, "Kevin, your problem is not a physical one. Your problem is a spiritual one. I don't make mistakes. Trust me?!" So I trusted the Lord and signed up for the summer mission trip instead. During a prayer time that week, one of the students shared about a woman who worked with her at the restaurant. The woman was suicidal because her baby was going to be born with Spina Bifida. She would most likely be paralyzed from the neck down. I was stunned and looked at my roommates with fear and trembling. I knew what I was supposed to do. I asked if she would ask this woman and her husband to meet with me.

They said yes.

When I walked into the restaurant, the couple was waiting anxiously. As I introduced myself, the mother kept staring at my legs, so I sat down next to them. I was nervous but also knew I was supposed to be there. They told me their story. I encouraged them that God doesn't make mistakes, and that he loved them. I didn't know what God was going to do with their daughter, but he had a plan for their whole family. It would be a hard road, but they could trust the Lord. They both gave their lives to Christ that day, and they invited me to the birth.

A few weeks later, they swung by my motel to pick me up. I jumped in the back of their old pickup and headed to Destin Beach. Their little girl was born with a huge four-inch hole in her back exposing her spinal cord with no protective vertebrae.

They invited me into the PICU. Her legs and arms were not moving, so I prayed over her. I am no miracle-worker, but her legs started to move and then her arms. Although she was missing her vertebrae and the external protective tissue, her spinal cord was fully intact.

The doctors began the process of stabilizing her spine and grafting the exposed area. I wasn't able to follow up with them, but that little girl changed my life forever. I realized for the first time that God had a plan for my Spina Bifida. He doesn't make mistakes.

The next week we were sharing our faith on the beach, and I came across a middle-aged man sitting by a pool. He saw me and asked if I was one of those Crusaders.

I chuckled and said, "I guess I am."

He went on to say, "I used to have faith, but I can no longer believe in God."

I asked him, "Why can't you believe in God anymore?"

He looked down at the ground and teared up, "I can't believe in a God that would take my six-year-old son."

I responded, "I'm so sorry. What happened to your son?" He said, "He died of Spina Bifida."

As I sat grieving with this man, I was also in awe of God's providence in putting us together.

I shared my story and the Gospel with this man who had lived in so much pain for so many years. He poured out his heart to me, and I leaned in and listened. I prayed with him and encouraged him that God set this meeting up for him to know that he never left him and has stored up every one of his tears. That he could turn back to him and entrust him with his future—a future of hope.

Posture: Faith
Identity: Neighbor, Servant

And he made from one man every nation of mankind to live on all the face of the earth, having determined allotted periods and the boundaries of their dwelling place, that they should seek God, and perhaps feel their way toward him and find him. Yet he is actually not far from each one of us.
Acts 17:26–27

If She Really Knows Me Will She Love Me?!

That summer, I heard my call to the ministry. I returned from my summer on the beach with a new zeal on life. I set my sights on Albania. It had been a closed nation to Christianity, but it opened up during my senior year. Idealistic visions of the mission field flowed through my veins, but it wasn't the only romance flowing through my veins.

Since I had made such a mess of relationships in the past, I had sworn off women.

Then I met Andrea.

Our mutual friend played matchmaker. She persuaded Andrea to go with her to the restaurant where her boyfriend worked to drop something off. I just happened to work there too.

After saying, "Hello," I proceeded to ask Andrea, "So what do you want to do with your life?" I was pretty intense at the time.

To my surprise, she answered, "I want to go on the mission field and tell people about Jesus."

I was taken off guard. What a woman! At that moment, I reconsidered my vow to swear off women. She was beautiful, sweet, loved Jesus, and wanted to go on the mission field!

As we grew in our friendship, my fears set in again, and the nagging question sunk back in my heart: "If she really knows me will she love me?!" Since there was only one way to find out, I asked her if she would attend a prayer event at the church with me. I made it clear that it was not a date but a prayer event. She said yes.

I was so nervous. I prayed before we got in the car. Prayed over our dinner. We fulfilled our hour slot of prayer for the twenty-four-hour prayer event at the church. I prayed while we roller skated afterwards (it was a date). And I prayed when I dropped her off at her dorm.

I quickly knew she was not any ordinary woman. It

wasn't long after that I shared about my Spina Bifida issues with her.

She leaned in, listened, and loved me well. My greatest fear had been conquered in one fell swoop. We didn't buy into the dating game, but we did settle with being "Friends with Potential." Our friendship tore down so many walls that we had erected in our lives due to previous broken relationships. We began to trust and hope again.

Posture: Faith
Identity: Beloved

There is no fear in love, but perfect love casts out fear. For fear has to do with punishment, and whoever fears has not been perfected in love. We love because he first loved us.
1 John 4:18–19

Kevin What Do You Do Just for Jesus without Anyone Seeing?!

Andrea moved around quite a bit before calling Aiken, South Carolina, home. She is the second daughter of four children. She has the sweetest smile. Her nose crinkles up, and her crystal blue eyes sparkle with the love of Christ. She started out a business major like me but shifted to education. She taught in the public school system, a private school, a few Christian schools, and ended up homeschooling all three of our children. (Oh, I let the cat out of the bag—we got married.)

Andrea came to know the Lord a year before me in the midst of transferring from the College of Charleston to the University of South Carolina. I like to think that God picked her up and placed her in Columbia for me, even though I know he had so many more purposes for her.

Andrea's love for the Bible and her kindness made her a faithful mentor for younger women. She has also ministered to many kids as a teacher. She still gets Christmas cards from the family of one of her initial first grade students. She led him to the Lord. This boy went on to lead his dad to the Lord which changed the trajectory of his family.

Andrea's zeal for justice leads her to fight for the unborn and women at risk.

I am most thankful for her deep, deep love for me as her husband. She has partnered with me with patience, forgiveness, and thankfulness as we serve the church together.

Before tying the knot, we thought we would end up on two different sides of the world on the mission field, but God's plans are not our plans. As I was moving forward with my conquest of Albania, my mother's brain tumor returned.

The tumor was lodged between her optical nerve and her pituitary gland and was robbing her of her sight and memory. I had to make a choice to go home and take care of her or go to Albania. I did what any son should do and went home to take care of my mom.

To be honest, it was a decision about either seeking a great name for myself on the mission field or to serve my mother, where no one was looking. God used that time to bring my ego under his banner of glory once again. During this time, God challenged me, "Kevin what do you do just for Jesus without anyone seeing?!"

Posture: Faith
Identity: Servant, Learner

But if anyone does not provide for his relatives, and especially for members of his household, he has denied the faith and is worse than an unbeliever.
1 Tim. 5:8

Kevin, You Know You're Not the Answer?!

God shaped my character in so many ways that year as he prepared me to be a husband and a father. While I was at home, I decided to find a job, a ministry and a way to be mentored. I started work at a five-star restaurant downtown. Ironically, the manager happened to be my old boss, the one who had got that hotel room for my friends back in high school. Remember the room that we trashed?

I asked for forgiveness and shared how I had come to know the Lord. He hired me on the spot. God is good.

I met with the pastor at my childhood church to see if they could use me in some way. They entrusted me with the college ministry, but I had larger plans to win the whole church for Christ—all three-thousand members. You can probably see by now how my zeal for the Lord gets tainted with my own pride.

God has to keep reminding me, "Kevin, you know you're not the answer?!" I also found out that there was a mission school nearby, where Aidan McKenzie had attended. He had discipled Adrian Depres. I met with the leader of the school, and he invited me to take classes without any cost.

During this time, Andrea and I travelled back and forth to visit each other. Six months in, I bought a ring to ask her to marry me. I just had to wait on the Lord's timing.

Posture: Faith

Identity: Learner, Worshiper, Culturemaker

But they who wait for the LORD shall renew their strength; they shall mount up with wings like eagles; they shall run and not be weary; they shall walk and not faint.
Is. 40:31

Why Me?!

My mom's surgery was set to be performed at the University of Virginia. As my mom and I boarded the plane, she threw up and got disoriented. She didn't recognize me.

I was desperate for the experimental Gamma Knife Treatment to help my mom. I was amazed at all the people at this medical center. People from all over the world seeking to be healed, to regain their sight and memory. Who were we that the Lord was mindful of us among these thousands of sufferers?

After prepping her for the surgery, I prayed over her and kissed her goodbye. I went for a walk in the housing quad at the University. It was night and there were parties cranking up in every dorm. I felt a bit cheated and complained to God, "Why me?! Lord, this is hard!. I'm a believer and struggling. All these students are having the time of their lives, and I'm here wondering if my mom is going to remember me or not?"

Posture: Arrogance
Challenged Identity: Entitled

Fret not yourself because of evildoers; be not envious of wrongdoers! For they will soon fade like the grass and wither like the green herb. Trust in the LORD, and do good; dwell in the land and befriend faithfulness. Delight yourself in the LORD, and he will give you the desires of your heart.
Ps. 37:1–4

Kevin, Where Have You Been?!

Trying to quiet the temptation to intoxicate my complaining heart, I wandered through a dark night of the soul for hours. I could hear Lady Folly screaming from the streets to escape, but by God's grace, I turned to the Lover of My Soul instead. After much time had passed, I entered back into my mom's room. To my surprise, she looked up at me with a smile and said, "Kevin, where have you been?!"

I felt like Adam when God asked him in the garden, "Where are you?"

My mom's memory and vision were immediately restored after the procedure, and the tumor has never returned. Once we got home, I would often hear her humming in the yard,

> Amazing Grace, How sweet the sound
> That saved a wretch like me
> I once was lost, but now am found,
> T'was blind but now I see.[9]

While my mom healed up, I continued to work, teach the college students, and attend classes. With the deeper life teaching from the mission school and my bent toward doing things in my own strength, I was steering the Sunday school class of college students down a man-centered path.

I thought they needed to be more faithful, more zealous, and more committed to the Lord. I was not teaching them about God's faithfulness and his preserving grace that undergirds our faith. A female Vanderbilt RUF (Reformed University Fellowship) student back home for summer break graciously asked me to read a book. It was *Putting Amazing Back into Grace* by Micheal Horton. I read it in two days and realized I had been teaching these students a works-righteousness, that God loved them for what they did for him, how they performed for him.

My mind was shifting toward a grace-centered theology, but practically I was urging them to live out their faith in their own strength. I started reading everything I could about sound theology. The pastors at the church noticed what I was reading and asked if I had considered seminary. They encouraged me to come under care of the presbytery. They would help send me to Princeton, Union, or Columbia Seminary. I asked if they would send me to Covenant Theological Seminary instead. I wanted to go to a school that believed the Bible and held to sound theology.

They said no.

I knew then that I couldn't come under their care, and I would need to find a church that I was fully aligned with.

Posture: Faith
Identity: Learner

All Scripture is breathed out by God and profitable for teaching, for reproof, for correction, and for training in righteousness, that the man of God may be complete, equipped for every good work.
2 Tim. 3:16–17

Go Get Her?!

My mom was back to her old self, and she gave me her blessing to pursue marriage. I decided to meet with Aidan McKenzie for an extensive prayer time about it— so I thought. I started to share my fears of my past to

Aidan, but he stopped me halfway through and said, "Let's just pray."

I said, "Well, okay."

Aidan began, "Lord, if you want Kevin and Andrea to get married then put them together quickly. If not. Tear them apart forever. AMEN!"

That was it! No long drawn out counseling session or prayer with fasting. Aidan had leaned in and listened to my heart for months. He knew I just needed a kick in the pants. I opened my eyes and knew that I loved Andrea with all my heart and couldn't imagine being ripped apart from her forever. Aidan gave me a manly Irish hug and said, "Go get her!"

Posture: Ignorance
Challenged Identity: Orphan

For God gave us a spirit not of fear but of power and love and self-control.
2 Tim. 1:7

Will You Marry Me?!

I set up a meeting with Andrea's dad to ask his blessing for her hand in marriage. Ironically, I took him to Po Folks restaurant for lunch. Even though I was a part-time waiter and didn't have a stable job, he gave me his blessing with tears in his eyes. He encouraged me to go and meet with their pastor since he would be doing the wedding. I told him not to tell anyone, because I had planned a special night the next week to ask her. He nodded in the affirmative, and I headed down the road to see if her pastor was in the office. We met for a good while and the conversation shifted from marriage to an interview for the youth ministry position at the church. I left Aiken with a blessing and a potential job offer.

Soon thereafter, I went over to Andrea's house and the phone rang. It was her mother, who was in England. Andrea began to talk with a strange look on her face.

Her mom asked her, "Is Nikki (Andrea's sister) pregnant?

Andrea said, "No I don't think so."

Andrea's mom went on, "Is she engaged?"

Andrea replied, "Not that I know."

Andrea's mom asked, "Are you engaged?"

Andrea said, "No!"

She then told Andrea that her dad had called and left a message with her grandfather that went something like, "Pappy Wally, Tell Trig (Andrea's Mom) that she is going to be a grandmother."

Andrea replied, "You know dad. He gets things mixed up and exaggerates."

Well, I was sitting there listening to this unfold and a bowling ball-sized gulp barreled down my throat and crashed into my stomach. I went out into the car and got the ring and came back in. When Andrea got off the phone, I got on my knees and said, "Well your dad didn't exaggerate this time. Will you marry me?!"

She was a bit taken back and asked, "Can we pray?"

Wisely, I let her do most of the praying and held off from pulling an Aidan on her. After a sweet moment of prayer, she said, "Yes." I got my first kiss that day too.

Later, God did lead me to be the youth pastor at New Covenant Presbyterian Church, a church in the Presbyterian Church in America, and they sent me to Covenant Theological Seminary and even paid my way.

Posture: Faith
Identity: Beloved, Neighbor

I am my beloved's, and his desire is for me.
Song of Sol. 7:10

His Story and My Story and Your Story Continues

Since those early days, Andrea and I have asked countless questions of our hearts both individually and together. The Lord has always been eager to listen and answer us. Many times, we asked in faith, but more times than not, our identity has been challenged due to swinging into ignorance and arrogance.

The Lord has never let us go though and has blessed us despite ourselves. We have been married for twenty seven years, and we have three wonderful children. We have served the church together in student ministry, ministry in a Korean church, church planting, community development, coordinating church planting, and other ventures. Some years were a delight and others a dilemma, but through it all God continued to shape our identity one degree of glory to the next.

As you noticed, there were many opportunities when my heart was asking tough questions, where I needed a friend in Christ. A believer willing to share his or her faith with his or her friends is crucial.

At different seasons in my life, seeds were planted along the way, but it wasn't until a friend leaned in, listened for, and loved me well that my heart was opened to the Good News of Jesus Christ.

Will you be that friend for someone? People are waiting for someone just like you to lean in, listen for, and love them well in Christ.

> *And Jesus went throughout all the cities and villages, teaching in their synagogues and proclaiming the gospel of the kingdom and healing every disease and every affliction. When he saw the crowds, he had compassion for them, because they were harassed and helpless, like sheep without a shepherd.*
> *Then he said to his disciples, "The harvest is plentiful, but the laborers are few; therefore pray earnestly to the Lord of the harvest to send out laborers into his harvest.*
> Matt. 9:35–38

> *So, being affectionately desirous of you, we were ready to share with you not only the gospel of God but also our own selves, because you had become very dear to us.*
> 1 Thess. 2:8

———

Hopefully, my next book will venture into my identity challenges as a Christian and Pastor focusing on the questions of the believer's heart with topics ranging from marriage, family, racism, prayer, failure, ministry, homosexuality, technology, finances, mercy, work, truth, aging parents, leisure, church, loss, leadership, and much more. After becoming a Christian, the questions of the heart keep on coming; therefore, we must keep in step with the Spirit. We must learn to walk in repentance and faith, coming to Jesus like a child fixing our eyes on the Author and Perfecter of our faith. Keep asking the questions of your heart. The Lord is listening and eager to answer.

---

1. Wendell Berry, *Jayber Crow* (Washington: Counterpoint, 2000), 29.
2. Charlie Peacock, *New Way to Be Human: A Provocative Look at What It Means to Follow Jesus* (Colorado Springs: Waterbrook Press, 2004), 90.
3. Edward T. Welch, *Side by Side: Walking with Others in Wisdom and Love* (Wheaton: Crossway, 2015), 97.
4. John Eldredge, *You Have What It Takes* (Nashville: Thomas Nelson Publishers, 2004), 7.
5. Tim Keller, *Counterfeit Gods: The Empty Promises of Money, Sex, and Power, and the Only Hope that Matters* (New York: Penguin Books, 2009), xviii.
6. *"The New Style,"* 1986, [cassette]. Track 2 on Beastie Boys, Licensed to Ill, Def Jam.
7. Joyce, Rachelle. "Quotes by Joyce Rachelle," accessed October 10, 2019. http://www.goodreads/quotes.
8. C. S. Lewis, "They Asked For A Paper," *Is Theology Poetry?* (London: Geoffrey Bless, 1962), 164–165.
9. John Newton, "Amazing Grace," 1779, #460, A Collection of Sacred Ballads, 1990.

OTHER EVANGELISTIC MODELS

Evangelism Explosion
https://evangelismexplosion.org

One Verse Evangelism
https://www.navigators.org/resource/one-verse-evangelism/

Roman Road
https://www.teenmissions.org/resources/roman-road-to-salvation/

Wordless Books & Bracelets
https://www.cefonline.com/about/history/wordless-book-discover-rich-heritage/

Christianity Explored
https://www.christianityexplored.org

The Life Book
https://thelifebook.com

Evangelize Today
https://www.evangelizetoday.info

Missional Communities
https://www.vergenetwork.org/2014/11/13/what-is-a-missional-community/

———

Go ahead and trust the Lord by leaning in, listening for, and loving well!

> *And Jesus came and said to them, "All authority in heaven and on earth has been given to me. Go therefore and make disciples of all nations, baptizing them in the name of the Father and of the Son and of the Holy Spirit, teaching them to observe all that I have commanded you. And behold, I am with you always, to the end of the age."*
> Matt. 28:18–20

> *But you will receive power when the Holy Spirit has come upon you, and you will be my witnesses in Jerusalem and in all Judea and Samaria, and to the end of the earth.* Acts 1:8

> *Therefore let it be known to you that this salvation of God has been sent to the Gentiles; they will listen. He*

lived there two whole years at his own expense, and welcomed all who came to him, proclaiming the kingdom of God and teaching about the Lord Jesus Christ with all boldness and without hindrance.

Acts 28:28–31

To follow along and join in,
please visit the author's website at

kevinthumpston.com

ALSO BY WHITE BLACKBIRD BOOKS

All Are Welcome: Toward a Multi-Everything Church

The Almost Dancer

Birth of Joy: Philippians

Choosing a Church: A Biblical and Practical Guide

Christ in the Time of Corona: Stories of Faith, Hope, and Love

Co-Laborers, Co-Heirs: A Family Conversation

Doing God's Work

EmbRACE: A Biblical Study on Justice and Race

Ever Light and Dark: Telling Secrets, Telling the Truth

Everything Is Meaningless? Ecclesiastes

Heal Us Emmanuel: A Call for Racial Reconciliation, Representation, and Unity in the Church

Hear Us, Emmanuel: Another Call for Racial Reconciliation, Representation, and Unity in the Church

The Organized Pastor: Systems to Care for People Well

Rooted: The Apostles' Creed

A Sometimes Stumbling Life

To You I Lift Up My Soul: Confessions and Prayers

Urban Hinterlands: Planting the Gospel in Uncool Places

Follow whiteblackbirdbooks.pub for titles and releases.

ABOUT WHITE BLACKBIRD BOOKS

White blackbirds are extremely rare, but they are real. They are blackbirds that have turned white over the years as their feathers have come in and out over and over again. They are a redemptive picture of something you would never expect to see but that has slowly come into existence over time.

There is plenty of hurt and brokenness in the world. There is the hopelessness that comes in the midst of lost jobs, lost health, lost homes, lost marriages, lost children, lost parents, lost dreams, loss.

But there also are many white blackbirds. There are healed marriages, children who come home, friends who are reconciled. There are hurts healed, children fostered and adopted, communities restored. Some would call these events entirely natural, but really they are unexpected miracles.

The books in this series are not commentaries, nor are they meant to be the final word. Rather, they are a collage of biblical truth applied to current times and places. The authors share their poverty and trust the Lord to use their words to strengthen and encourage his people. Consider these books as entries into the discussion.

May this series help you in your quest to know Christ as he is found in the Gospel through the Scriptures. May you look for and even expect the rare white blackbirds of God's redemption through Christ in your midst. May you be thankful when you look down and see your feathers have turned. May you also rejoice when you see that others have been unexpectedly transformed by Jesus.